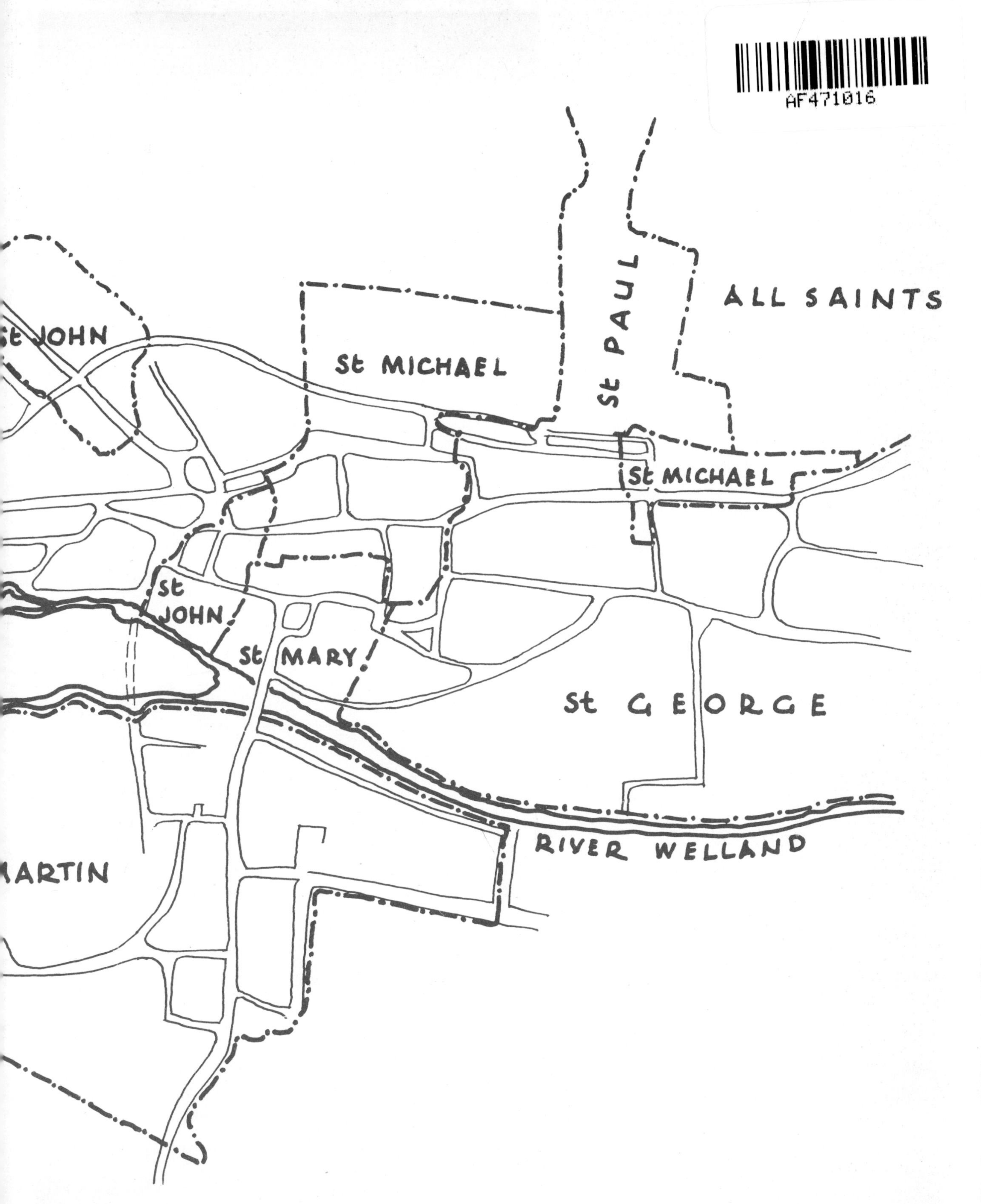

St JOHN
St MICHAEL
St PAUL
ALL SAINTS
St MICHAEL
St JOHN
St MARY
St GEORGE
MARTIN
RIVER WELLAND
AF471016

BARRACUDA BOOKS

The Book of Stamford 1983
has been published as a Limited
Edition of which this is

Number 261

A complete list of the original
subscribers is printed at the
back of the book

THE BOOK OF STAMFORD

FRONT COVER: The last cattle market — in Broad Street, 1896.

View of Stamford from the Meadows. (JD)

THE BOOK OF STAMFORD

BY

ALAN ROGERS MA DPhil

BARRACUDA BOOKS LIMITED
BUCKINGHAM, ENGLAND
MCMLXXXIII

PUBLISHED BY BARRACUDA BOOKS LIMITED
BUCKINGHAM, ENGLAND
AND PRINTED BY
HOLYWELL PRESS LIMITED
OXFORD, ENGLAND

BOUND BY
GREEN STREET BINDERY LIMITED
OXFORD, ENGLAND

JACKET PRINTED BY
CHENEY & SONS LIMITED
BANBURY, OXON

LITHOGRAPHY BY
BICESTER PHOTOLITHO LIMITED
BICESTER, ENGLAND

DISPLAY SET IN BASKERVILLE
AND TEXT SET IN 11/12pt BASKERVILLE BY
HARPER PHOTOTYPESETTERS LIMITED
NORTHAMPTON, ENGLAND

ISBN 0 86023 123 2

Contents

Acknowledgements

This book owes a great deal to a large number of persons with whom I have worked over the last twenty or more years. They are too numerous for me to name them all, but special mention must be made of the following: all the members, past and present, of the Stamford Survey Group who taught me so much; the staff of the Stamford Archaeological Research Committee and its successor bodies, and the staff of the Royal Commission on Historical Monuments; the Trustees of Browne's Hospital and the various parish incumbents of the town; Stamford Public Library and especially the town's former librarian, Laurie Tebbutt. Much help and constant friendship have come from the following: Chris Davies, Mike Key, Dick Grimwood, Garry Till, Dr E. C. Till, Archie Ireson, John Chandler, Phil Roberts, Canon J P. Hoskins, Professor W. G. Hoskins, Ann Mathews and many, many others. The county archivists of Lincolnshire and Northamptonshire and their staff have proved perpetually helpful. Most of the illustrations come from the collection of the Stamford Survey Group, but some derive from drawings in the British Library collections, in private hands, or elsewhere. Phil Roberts and Dermott Francis assisted with the line drawings. To them all, I am most grateful.

Key to Caption Credits

Stamford is a much-drawn and much-photographed town; and large numbers of original and reproduced illustrations survive. The illustrations chosen for this book come mainly from the extensive collections of J. C. Chandler and the Stamford Survey Group, as well as from the author's own collection. Some have been taken for this work. Originals are acknowledged as follows:

BL	British Library's collections (Twopeny, Buckler and Blore drawings).
DF	Drawings by Dermot Francis.
JD	John Dolby
JSH	John S. Hartley's collection of Montagu Jones' drawings.
LT	Laurence Tebbutt's collection.
MP	Mrs. M. Peart's collection of Nattes' drawings and Traylen's photographs.
PR	Drawn by P. R. Roberts (Stamford).
PRO	Public Record Office.
SLHS	Stamford Local History Society (formerly the Stamford and Rutland Archaeological and Local History Society).
SM	*Stamford Mercury*.
TH	Town Hall collection of paintings etc.

Foreword
by J. P. Hoskins

'Stamford is a peach of a town' wrote one of the reviewers of the Royal Commission on Historical Monuments' volume, *The Town of Stamford.* All who know and love Stamford, and to know it is to love it, will agree that the description is both apt and charming. Few are the places that have so much treasure, architectural and historical, as is to be found in this silvery grey casket in its green and lovely setting in the valley of the Welland.

The splendid buildings of Stamford, displaying as they do a continuous, fine tradition from the eleventh century virtually to the present day, speak of the mediaeval and later importance and prosperity of the place. They tell also of the love and pride of its people in their town. It is of a piece with this that so much has been affectionately if not always quite accurately written about the history of Stamford during the past three centuries — most of it by those who have lived in it, or nearby — beginning with Richard Butcher, a native and former town clerk, whose *Survey and Antiquities of the Towne of Stamford* of 1646 is one of the very earliest of such town histories.

Now it is a privilege and a pleasure to welcome the latest of these, *The Book of Stamford,* by Dr Alan Rogers. During the past twenty years or more Professor Rogers has, happily for Stamford, devoted much of his time and expert scholarship to its history. He has also encouraged and guided the studies of others and, in particular, of the members of the Stamford Survey Group. The appearance of *The Book of Stamford* is therefore warmly to be greeted, and will be, as an authoritative, important and delightful contribution to the historiography of this 'peach of a town'.

J. P. Hoskins.

Preface
by Lady Leatham

The town of Stamford is a national treasure. It is part of the English heritage, one of those features which help to make England the special place that it is. The buildings, the Meadows, the bridge and the river, the town walls, all go together to make one of the most pleasant towns in the country. Its history is in many ways an epitome of the history of the realm, an illustration of all the major trends and events which have occurred in these islands. Without Stamford and other towns like it, England would be the poorer.

But Stamford is not just a pretty place; it is a living community of people. Those who have resided in the town in the past have contributed to its history and left their mark behind; and those who now live here are keenly interested in what they see around them. They are caring for the town, learning about it and recording it for posterity. Many families, like our own, have been in the town for many generations; others are more or less recent arrivals. This has been true of all periods of Stamford's history. But both groups are equally Stamfordians, both are equally interested in learning about the history of the town and in preserving it.

This book will contribute much to this process. Its story which tells of how Stamford developed, both as a regional market town and at times one of the country's major towns, helps to explain much that we see around us; and the illustrations will help to make us more aware of what survives and needs to be preserved. It is a valuable addition to the many accounts of Stamford's history and deserves to sell well.

Stamford's antiquarian image: the sign reads 'Stay Awhile Amid Its Ancient Charm'.

Dedication

This book is dedicated to all my friends and former colleagues
in the Stamford Survey Group, 1965-1979.

ABOVE: Stukeley note book. (SLHS) LEFT: Portrait of William Stukeley. RIGHT: Portrait of Francis Peck.

The Basis of the Past

> Why compose a history book when all you have to do is to copy
> the best-known ones, as is the custom? If you have a new view,
> an original idea, if you exhibit men and things in an unexpected
> light, you will surprise the reader. And the reader does not like to
> be surprised. He looks in a history book for the legends he knows
> already. If you try to teach him, you will do nothing but humiliate
> and annoy him. Do not try to enlighten him or he will exclaim that
> you are attacking his beliefs. So copy one another and thereby save
> yourselves fatigue and avoid appearing over-weening.
>
> *Anatole France*

It all began with Bladud, in 863 BC or rather, in the year 3100 *anno mundi*.

Prince Bladud, you will remember, was the father of King Lear and son of King Hudibras, a direct descendant of that Brutus who founded the kingdom of Britain, or Albion. This prince was a clever lad who travelled widely; he returned to Greece, the land of his forefathers (for Brutus was of course descended from Aeneas of the Trojan War fame) and there he learned (or according to some authorities taught) in the schools of Athens for a time. On the death of his father, he returned to Britain, bringing some of his teachers back with him so as to set up a school in his new realm:

> When at Athens he had studied clear
> He brought with him four philosophers wise,
> School to hold in Britain and exercise.

Once established on the throne, he and his companions looked about for some suitable place in which to establish a centre of learning similar to the Greek academy of his youth; and they settled on Stamford:

> At last they found a place therefore.
> Amidst the realm it lies welnigh . . . .
> An healthful place, not low nor high,
> An wholesome soil for their behove;
> With water streams, and springs for wells,
> And meadows sweet, and valleys green,
> And woods, grove, quarries, all things else,
> For students' weal or pleasure been.

In this place, Bladud established a university:

> He built the schools, like Attic's then
> And gave them lands to maintain those
> Who were accounted learned men,
> And could the grounds of arts disclose.
> The town is called Stamford yet . . . .

Such was the story of 'the beginning' of Stamford, a myth from antiquity, already strong in the fifteenth century and elaborated by later writers. It is true that the early sixteenth century antiquarian Leland dismisses the legend as 'a dream', and that Francis Peck in reciting it at length two centuries later is honest enough to admit that 'it requires great judgement to distinguish and part out what is truth, when it is bewrapt and clouded with such an heap of fictions'; but he still allows the story to stand, and from him it has passed into the mythology of the town.

Such an account of the town's origin, cherished by generations of writers, reveals two of the main characteristics of the inhabitants of this East Midlands market town — their antiquarianism and their gentility.

The antiquarianism of Stamford has an ancient history. It may in fact go back into the later Middle Ages; it certainly dates from the mid-seventeenth century, when Richard Butcher (a former town-clerk, dismissed from his office in highly political circumstances) wrote one of the earliest urban histories of the country. He it was who first drew the attention of his fellow townsmen to the physical remains from the past around them — the churches, houses and fragments of mediaeval religious buildings which survived from earlier days. It is quite clear that in much of what he wrote he was drawing heavily on long-standing traditions in the town, some of them well-founded, some garbled. And from his day to our own, Stamford has never lacked its own home-produced antiquarian, the collector of trifles and interpreter of dreams. And the interest is general, not confined to the few; even the last members of the recently demised borough council, in their roadside signs urging visitors to spend time (and of course money) in the town, employed antique phrasing — and vocabulary: 'Stay awhile amidst its ancient charms'.

The antiquarian interests of Stamfordians are thus of long standing. Richard Butcher, town clerk, innkeeper and gentleman, was succeeded by an apothecary and gentleman, 'poor old Howgrave, the Topographer of Stamford', and by the Reverend Francis Peck; they in turn by Harrod (whose two volumes of 1785 were described as 'certainly amusing . . . with no ostentatious pretentions'), Drakard, Burton, Nevinson, Justin Simpson, Tickell and so on. They were printers, clergy, lawyers and the like. When Justin Simpson, arguably the best of Stamford's nineteenth century antiquarians, wrote in one of his notebooks about Henry Boor, son of 'old Joe Boor, chimneysweep' in glowing terms —

'was for many years booking clerk at the George Hotel in the palmy old coaching days and subsequently in the service of the L. and N.W. Railway company. He collected a good topographical library and also a no mean collection of coins. I am glad to place here on permanent record my obligation for many acts of kindness received that tended much to foster my taste for antiquities, etc'.

— he was describing a type by no means unknown in Stamford in other areas. Joseph Phillips (1824-1907), town clerk and solicitor for much of the nineteenth century, made an extensive collection of historical and contemporary literature, much of which came on his death into the possession of the town; and the coin collections of the publisher Sharp and of Colson, together with the tokens assiduously mustered by Justin Simpson, ended up in the town hall as well.

Historical accounts of Stamford came off the presses with regularity throughout the late eighteenth and nineteenth centuries. Most of these histories and chronologies are, it is true, derivative — expansive but derivative. Howgrave's work of 1725, for instance, 'was only a republication of Butcher with some alterations and additions', as was stated on the death of Howgrave in 1771. Fact and fantasy were thus copied indiscriminately and enlarged upon; small stories grew into tall ones. Each new addition confirmed the outline and paved the way for the next.

And much of the basis of this tradition lay in the material fabric that made up Stamford. Fragments of mediaeval stonework were for instance lovingly cherished and carefully transported from place to place, in turn giving rise to new lengends. It is perhaps not altogether strange that the serious and systematic study of Stamford's past, its archaeology, buildings and records, should only have begun in the 1960s; too much was at stake for generations of Stamford historians for it to have started earlier.

In view of this long tradition, it is not surprising that Stamfordians should have traced their origins to some legendary British prince. But that it took the form of his establishment of a university is also typical. For Stamford is nothing if not a genteel town. The story appealed to the clergy and professional men who wrote about the town's past precisely because it did not threaten their way of life. Not for them the dirty story of Bladud and his herd of swine wallowing in the mud, a story which marks the origins of that prince's other alleged urban foundation, Bath. The town cherished its academic pretentions for many a century. Leland, writing in Henry VIII's reign, comments on the number of large halls or houses in the town which some of the residents ascribed to an earlier but defunct university, legends which Leland gently doubted. The height of this gentility came in the early eighteenth century with the residence in Stamford of that arch-antiquarian the Reverend Dr William Stukeley, physician and clergyman. He it was who fully developed the traditions, ascribing house after house to 'colleges' of the University, until his friend and supporter in these flights of fancy, Francis Peck, gently poked fun at his imaginings by calling this vicar of All Saints 'President of Black Hall, Peterborough Hall, Sempringham Hall, Durham Hall and Vaudey Hall'.

But in fact, things are not always what they seem in Stamford; the gentility is often only surface-deep. Thus the houses of the town so often hide behind later fronts (mostly of Georgian style) of much earlier buildings. So the Whitefriars' site is really that of the Greyfriars, and that of the Greyfriars is the Whitefriars. And similarly it is with Stamford's historians — they are frequently misleading. Butcher's *Survey and Antiquities of Stamford,* for instance, was a political tract relating to the internal disputes in the borough's government rather than a local history. Howgrave's *History* (1725), published in a sense of rivalry and exasperation just before Peck's major book appeared two years later, was apparently written by one Curtis, according to Michael Tyson of Cambridge: 'Amongst others who were tired of waiting for it [ie Peck's long-promised volume] was my grandfather Curtis, who put together that book to which Howgrave lent his name. Howgrave wrote the preface; it was done only to plague Peck'. Even Peck's *magnum opus* (1727) was not just re-arranged (and, according to Stukeley, 'spoiled') at the instance of others; much of it was compiled by Zacchary Grey and other antiquarians. A good deal of Harrod's work (1785) was written by John Lowe, a surgeon and apothecary of Stamford, 'a facetious companion'; while Drakard's *Survey* (1822) was the work of either Octavius Gilchrist or Thomas Blore. Even more recent writers have sheltered behind their publishers. In this, of course, the eighteenth or nineteenth century writers on Stamford's past were not unusual; what does call for remark is the large number of such cases among the published histories of one town.

And so the traditions and the misunderstandings have continued to the present — the antiquarianism and the gentility, with all the accumulated weight of legend and misunderstanding of more than three hundred years of writings. The sense of the past which coloured so many of the actions of earlier Stamfordians is still strong — stronger perhaps than the desire for accuracy. The recently erected and totally unfounded inscription in memory of Queen Boadicea chasing the Roman troops over Stamford Meadows bears witness to this tendency, as does the persistent search for a mythical parish church dedicated to St Thomas. In 1961, the borough chose to face the challenge that a new bypass posed to local trade by celebrating one year early the 500th anniversary of a borough charter granted in 1462 — on the grounds that the calendar year had been altered in 1752 and that the original grant had been made in February 1461/2! Similarly in 1972, the council planned extensive festivities to mark the millenium of 'the town's first charter', in the face of the knowledge that the alleged charter of 972 (in fact, a post-Conquest forgery) was ganted by King Edgar not to the borough but to Peterborough Abbey and merely mentioned the name of Stamford in passing. Even the BBC itself could be misled into alleging — quite inaccurately — that Stamford was a university town before Oxford or Cambridge. And the gentility also survives. Concerned at the threat of redevelopment and full of fears about industrial growth in the region, the borough council revived the town's claim to a university; the case it made to the government in 1962 was a strong one. What lay behind it may seem to some to have been a feeling that a university was ' a form of clean development', an acceptable face of modern society; and it is noticeable that as the student's public image declined in the disorders of the later 1960s, the claim was pressed less and less fervently. In this, the people of Stamford were as true to their past as to their present character.

And this character has resulted in real and positive achievements. The past of the town may have more than its fair share of legends, still firmly accepted; the town may still fear to face the challenge of industrial and post-industrial Britain. But the strong concern of the inhabitants of this town to preserve its past has resulted in a unique collection of old buildings, in a townscape arguably second to none in Europe. And it is to be hoped that now that the decisions about the town's development are — for the first time for more than six hundred years — being taken outside the town, those who decide about the future of Stamford will aim to preserve the best of both its gentility and the signs of its antiquity. Ony time will tell and thus far the first signs to not augur well.

View of Stamford from the south.

ABOVE: The river at Stamford has played a large part in the town's history. BELOW: The earliest crossing into the town across the Meadows' marked by the George bridge (right), the causeway and the Lammas bridge (left, distance). (JD)

LEFT: Lammas bridge and entry into the old town. RIGHT: Lammas bridge and pool with main bridge in background. BELOW: The mediaeval bridge and main entry to town; the George and Angel is at the top of St Mary's Hill, blocking the way ahead. (MP)

Setting and Origins

In the little Volume of this Book
With judgement's Eye who so shall please
  to look;
Such various learning he therein shall
  find
As shall express the Author's Glorious
  Mind:
The Scite of *Stamford,* in Rhetorick straine,
  Set forth:

Thomas Seamer, congratulating
Richard Butcher, 1646

Bladud's four philosophers were sent out to find a suitable site for their university — and in the middle of the realm they foud their 'sylvan ideal', with a wholesome soil, an adequate water supply in streams and wells, sweet meadows, green valleys, woods and groves, quarries and all other necessities for the health and pleasure of the students. And if to some this paradise seems overwritten, then they have never in fact visited Stamford.

It is not, of course, in the middle of the realm; but it is almost exactly half-way between London and the Humber. It is thirty odd miles to the sea at Boston and a little more to King's Lynn (though of course the coastline, the river mouths and the ports have all changed frequently over the past thousand years or so) and, at about the same distance to the west, lies the ancient Midlands centre of Leicester. Stamford thus lies at the centre of a wide and varied region, with rich fenlands to the east, forest and heathland to the south and north, and the fertile central lowland plains not far away on the west. 'Not too high nor too low' it certainly is; on the eastern edge of the limestone hills, facing over the fens, it avoids the extremes of both.

But the origins of Stamford owe more to its immediate site than to its general setting — and in this, it is quite clear that the factors that influenced Bladud's philosophers also determined those first Anglo-Saxons or Vikings who settled on the spot. The soil is indeed wholesome — a mixture of boulder clay sweetened by the limestone which underlies the clay at various depths. Stamford stands on that belt of Jurassic limestone which sweeps across England in a broad curve from south-west to north-east — a belt which constitutes at one end the broad Cotswold region and at the other end the narrow Cliff north of Lincoln. In places the limestone lies close to the surface, much striated by frost and erosion. In other places, the clay is deep — and useful in its own right, for pottery and brick and tile making, among other things.

But clearly the most important feature of Stamford's development was its water supply, its streams and wells. The town, as the name (originally *Stanford,* ie *Stony-ford*) implies, lies in one of the river valleys that cut into the eastern face of the limestone belt. At the point where Stamford stands, the river Welland flows from the uplands of Rockingham Forest down into the fens. The river is clearly an important one — the boundary between counties for much of its length. It is the middle river of three, with the Nene lying to the south and the Gwash, with its tributaries, to the north. And it was at the crossing of this river that Stamford grew up.

The river has consistently played a large part in the town's history — as transport route, power supply, sewer and the like. It flooded regularly and often excessively, much to the disgust of the residents at the bottom of St Mary's Street and High Street, St Martin's. But it does not seem to have served so prominently as a source for water. For this, the town was well supplied with springs and wells. Most of the parishes had their own well; so did many private individuals. The mediaeval friars, the monks at St Leonards and the town council had conduits, bringing drinking water into the town from springs in the fields just north or south of the town — in Emlyn Close or at East-Well-Head, among others. Of course the mediaeval inhabitants had to be restrained from polluting the wells by washing dirty clothes in them — they were only allowed to do this on certain days. But this perhaps reflects the certainty of Stamford residents that they were well endowed with nature's choicest gift, plenty of good clean water.

Bladud's philosophers saw meadows and green valleys. Riverside meadows, lying between two branches of the Welland, are as much a feature of Stamford as they are of Oxford. They have been carefully preserved over the generations and now seem assured in perpetuity. Their green contrasts with the yellow-grey of the stone buildings which line the sides of the valley. They lie immediately to the west of the bridge which crosses the river after its two branches have re-united. Just for a short distance, the valley narrows, trapping the Meadows above the junction; and it was at this narrowest point that the present bridge was built, close to the ford which gave the town its name, at the highest navigable point on the river — a site chosen both for defence and access to the crossing.

Green valleys, woods and groves lay round the town. Rolling heathland, deep cut valleys (those mainly to the north having been cut off by the glaciers of the Ice Age, which accounts for their north-south alignment) and woodland still mark the surrounding countryside. Rockingham Forest lay to the south-west, the forest that gave Kesteven its name lay to the north; both areas today still show a heavy cover of woodland. Even towards the fens, there lay forest, as the famous *Anglo-Saxon Chronicle* records; for the Saxon monks of Peterborough, upset by the appointment of a Norman abbot over them, were alleged to have seen huntsmen, 'black, huge and hideous, who rode on black horses and on he-goats, and their hounds were jet black, with eyes like saucers, and horrible . . . in all the woods that stretch from that same town to Stamford'. And finally there were — and still are — the quarries, for the Jurassic limestone in and around Stamford made excellent building material. The names of Barnack and Clipsham (famous in building history for the quality of their stone) are enough to reveal the importance of these sites, while further north the Ancaster quarries, along with these other two places, supplied many of the cathedrals and castles of eastern England with their products.

Stamford had thus many local advantages: like the Jewish Canaan, it was 'a good land, a land of brooks of water, of fountains and deep pools, springing forth in valleys and hills; a land of wheat and barley . . . a land whose stones are iron, and out of whose hills you can dig brass'. There was good barley land at Stamford on the heath, and cornland in the valleys. To the west lay the ironstone which was certainly used by the Romans and later gave rise to Corby and the unsightly quarries south of Grantham. Only the brass (excusable poetic licence) is missing.

In view of all this, it is perhaps surprising that settlement came to Stamford so late — for of course Bladud's philosophers lay only in the imaginings of the fifteenth-century poet John Harding and his fellow myth-makers. There are no signs of anything permanent on the site of Stamford before the coming of the Anglo-Saxons into the land. The absence of both pre-historic and Roman settlements is puzzling. For the Welland valley on either side of Stamford is thick with pre-historic and Roman sites. Both sides of the lower Welland valley were densely settled by the time the Romans came, as air photographs and excavation in advance of gravel quarrying have shown. One of the most densely and persistently occupied of all parts of England lay to the east around Maxey, Tallington and the Deepings, and the sites spread all along the valley until they reached the outskirts of Stamford itself (a Bronze Age site on the Barnack Road, to the south-east of the town, was recently discovered) — but not at Stamford itself, despite the fact that the site must have been the first crossing point available to the inhabitants of both sides of the river.

The crossing of the river, too, was important in other ways. The long overland trek of the pre-historic Briton, from south-west to north-east, lay along the top of the limestone ridge; and this trackway seems to have crossed the Welland at several points — including Stamford, where it joined another pre-historic route known later as Sewstern Lane and running from the Welland Valley settlements (and perhaps East Anglia) to a similar area of dense pre-historic population in the Trent Valley near Newark. But despite all of this, there seems to have been no early settlement at or near Stamford. The intensive occupation of later generations with much excavation for cellars and refuse pits may have destroyed signs of pre-Saxon settlement: but this is unlikely to have been total.

A similar puzzle, too, faces us with the Romans. The great road of Imperial Britain from the south coast to the north ran across the Welland at a point near where the town of Stamford later grew up, but without any known Roman setlement there. Their main defended points lay on the Nene to the south (at Water Newton) and on the Gwash to the north (at Casterton), but not at Stamford. Some few Romans finds have from time to time been made in the town — coins, urns and other pottery, and even fragments of an alleged pavement near the bridge; it is possible (indeed, probable, I think) that the valley still hides some Roman villa in the immediate neighbourhood of the town — but it is certain that there was no town or major settlement on this site then. Casterton was the main centre of population during the period of the Roman occupation and indeed in the earliest days of the Saxon settlement.

When did the site of Stamford first become settled? We don't know for certain. A Saxon cemetery to the east of the town may indicate an early settlement in or near the town. Bede (in about 732) refers to a Stamford in existence in about 658, and it is possible (but on the whole unlikely) that this was our Stamford. The name itself (which may of course originally have referred to a settlement or equally to the ford alone) could have been coined at any time before the Scandinavians landed and settled in the middle of the ninth century. It has been suggested that the Welland ford lay within the territory of the Roman town of Casterton and formed part of the first 'Rutland' from which it came to be separated, perhaps by the Danes soon after their settlements in this area, but this is a guess (though eminently reasonable).

All that we do know for sure is that by 918 Stamford was already a place of some importance. A mention of the ford in 894 still does not necessarily indicate a town or indeed any settlement at all; and indeed it may have been the Danes, entering by the Wash and the river Welland, who chose and fortified the site for the first time, but this is unlikely. Certainly it was a focal point well before 918, for in the early summer of that year, King Edward of Wessex, in his attacks on the Danish settlers, 'marched with his levies to Stamford, and had a fortress built on the south bank of the river; all the people who owed allegiance to the more notherly fortress submitted to him and sought him for their lord' (*Anglo-Saxon Chronicle*). He stayed there for some time until the death of his sister Ethelflaed, Lady of Mercia, took him away to Tamworth and the business of consolidating his newly-won kingdom.

Thus Stamford emerges onto the pages of history, already a town with apparently something of a past attached to it. A possible Anglo-Saxon settlement around a ford over the Welland may have become under the Danes an important military site, defended against its enemies and apparently the centre of a region — one of the Five Boroughs of the Danelaw.

> 'The Boroughs Five he won, Leicester and Lincoln
> Nottingham, Derby and Stamford too,'

sang the Anglo-Saxon Chronicler. Perhaps it is not quite true to say that Stamford was the *centre* of a region, for it is clear that all those who lived south of the river owed allegiance even in those days to Northampton; the river was the frontier. Stamford's dependent territory lay to the west and to the north of the river, and when the town fell to the king of Wessex, then the people of its appendant land came over to the conqueror too.

This raises the whole problem of 'Stamfordshire', a problem too complicated to be dealt with in depth here. Suffice it to say that the map suggests that there once was (or ought to have been) a shire dependent on Stamford, and that it lay (or ought to have lain) north of the town, similar to Northamptonshire, to Cambridge's, Huntingdon's and Nottingham's shires, and that there is an occasional passing reference to a Stamfordshire. But whether the intention was ever carried out (indeed whether it even existed) is not certain. For the Norse invaded and swept over Yorkshire and the lands of the Five Boroughs. Stamford once again fell under the control of a Scandinavian king, and it has indeed been argued (on rather flimsy coin evidence) that in the 950s the town became the seat of the Norse 'king' Anlaf. But Edward son of Edmund once more rescued the town and the others of the Five Boroughs from the hand of the invader and in the subsequent redistribution of territory, the lands formerly dependent upon Stamford went to support Lincoln with its double territory.

But the town survived, and clearly grew in importance. Whether its Danish defences lasted long after 918 (as they did at Nottingham) is not certain, but probably they did, for by about 940 Stamford had become a mint town, and it may be argued that only towns with some measure of protection would be used for such a purpose. Indeed, if we judge by the number of coiners known to have been at work between the reign of Aethelred and Edward the Confessor (although this number may be distorted by the chance find of a large hoard of coins near Oakham in 1749, a hoard which contained many examples from Stamford), the Stamford mint was one of the most important in the realm for a century or more before William the Conqueror arrived, much more important than all the others of the Five Boroughs except Lincoln and probably fifth in the whole kingdom. There are signs too of iron-working in the town at this time, while perhaps more significantly the town developed a distinctive pottery industry early too. This is now more certain than it was a few years ago; recent excavations have revealed how early that form of pottery known as 'Stamford ware' was first made and how long it lasted.

It was certainly being made in the town, from local clay (perhaps from the present Williamson Cliff site on the ridge to the north of the town, for as late as the nineteenth century there were complaints that various inhabitants were carrying away soil from this site for their own purposes) from the late ninth century, and at least nine kiln sites have now been identified. With its clear white fabric and later its pleasing early green glaze, it proved popular throughout the whole of eastern England and indeed more widely, throughout the newly united kingdom and even on the continent. Stamford had begun its long career as an international trading centre.

It is perhaps this characteristic of the early town which helps to account for the shape of mediaeval Stamford. One of the most noticeable features of the old town (now of course the present town centre) is its east-west orientation, a surprising characteristic for those who see Stamford as a creation of the north-south road system. It is clear that the shape of ancient Stamford was moulded by the river, not the road. It stood at the highest navigable point on the Welland. All its east-west roads are wide and level, lying along the terraces of the valley; all its north-south routes consist of short narrow lanes, often with sharp bends or abrupt ends to them. Clearly the town lay on an important east-west route running along the north side of river; the mills along the river and the wharves below the ford helped to create the distinctive shape of the early town, and the ford provided the settlements lower down the valley with their first crossing and a route into East Anglia or the East Midlands.

The small fortified Danish settlement would seem to have lain within a quadrilateral still indicated by the sharp corners of St Mary's Street – St John's Street to the south-west and of Broad Street and Star Lane (greatly widened in the 1930s) to the north-east. St Michael's and perhaps St Andrew's churches lay in this area, and one of these may have existed before William the Conqueror arrived. To the west, outside this Danish nucleus, stood a market area around All Saints Church, which may or may not have pre-dated the Danish fortified town; a bit further west again, on the other side of a stream (marked now by a culvert) which flowed down Scotgate, Mallory Lane and Castle Dyke into the Welland, was another area, more lightly settled and later to become the castle with the church of St Peter, again probably pre-Conquest. These two foci laid the basis for the growth of the mediaeval town. A suburb grew up south of the river, but it did not take its final form until the ford had been replaced by a bridge. Stamford thus came to represent a capital letter T, with the east-west route having priority in chronology and in importance over the north-south route; it is this which accounts for the sharp bends in the line of the Great North Road at the top of St Mary's Hill and again at St John's Street. Only the east-west part of the town on the north side of the river became incorporated into the walled area of the later borough, not the part of the town which stretched to the south of the Welland.

Thus was created Stamford, probably by the late Anglo-Saxons and enlarged by the Danes, along the river which was to continue to be so important in the life of the town. Despite legends, going back at least to Leland's day, that 'it was a borrow towne in Kynge Edgares dayes', it is not known to have received any pre-Conquest Royal charters. Nevertheless, it was already an important urban community with pottery, coining, marketing and perhaps iron smelting at the heart of its activities. Defended, industrialised, a centre of trade, it faced the new age of the Normans on secure foundations.

And yet the seeds of failure were already there. It had failed to secure its own shire and thus was relegated to a peripheral position in the regionalisation of the realm. In periods when Stamford was able to create for itself a distinctive national role or a range of social activities for the region, it grew in importance; when it failed to do this it declined, becoming a small market town mid-way between the villages and the larger urban centres around it. The see-saw that was Stamford's history had begun.

The river provided power for several mills, notably The King's Mill,

ABOVE: Hudd's Mill, which belonged to the corporation. BELOW: The river flooded regularly: view from Town Hall to the west across the Meadows. (SM)

24

ABOVE: The mid-Lent fair on Bath Row during the floods. (SM)
BELOW: The town was formerly surrounded by windmills.

The road to the east viewed from St Michael's church — a main thoroughfare.

ABOVE: Stamford pottery, glazed and unglazed, eleventh and twelfth century. (Differing reductions from actual size) (LT) BELOW: Coins from Stamford mint, Anglo-Saxon period. (DF)

ABOVE: Fragments of Norman stone houses. RIGHT: St Peter's Street. LEFT: St Mary's Hill. BELOW: St Paul's church (twelfth century): early print.

Heights of Glory, 1100-1300

E. A., 1646

Some twenty years after William the Conqueror landed and defeated the 'usurper' on the throne of England, Royal commissioners descended on the town of Stamford, to survey it on behalf of the King, together with the rest of the realm, and to write up their findings in the Domesday Book. What sort of a place did they find at Stamford then?

It is possible that the town was rather less important in 1086 than it had been some hundred years earlier. Nevertheless, the picture that can be drawn from the record contained in the Domesday Survey is one of a town with all the characteristics of a 'county' town but without that status. The 'royal borough' of Stamford comprised some 2,000 or 3,000 inhabitants, mixed in population, both English and Danes sharing equally in a common economy. Some of the greatest people in the realm held property in the town, including Edward the Confessor's queen, Edith (who held nearby Hambleton — now in Rutland — and with it an estate in Stamford consisting at the least of several houses and a church, St Peter's) and Countess Judith, the Conqueror's niece. But most of the inhabitants were of humbler status. Some were dependent on neighbouring manors, set in the town to buy and sell on behalf of their overlords, while others were freemen, free to buy and sell, to leave their property to their heirs without interference.

In some ways the town had changed little. It still had a market; and the coiners, if not so active, nevertheless still held a prized right. The chief men in the town were still the Danish 'lawmen', a group of property owners who interpreted, preserved and passed on the borough customs. Part of the town had come to be dominated (rather loosely at first) by the Abbot of Peterborough, but otherwise Stamford was still free of close domination by any great lord, despite the presence of the Queen's property there.

But in some ways the town had been changed by the recent events. It is possible that the Norman conquerors brought into Stamford (as they did at Nottingham and elsewhere) a number of French settlers, with their own market place (an area called in the Domesday Book Portland) lying between All Saints and St Peter's churches; it may be significant that a prominent Saxon landlord, Ernuin the priest, who not only retained most of his estates but also acquired other property after the Conquest, lost all his extensive possessions in Stamford. Certainly William the Conqueror himself ordered a castle to be built just beside the town and above the river — and built it was, destroying in the process some five houses. And this is interesting, because Stamford was the only non'-county' town in which the new King established a fortress within a year or two of the battle of Hastings, a fact which reflects its status as a semi-county town and which may support other indications that the Queen had had a 'hall' in the town before the Conquest, part of her dowry estate of Rutland. It was a relatively small castle, with an artificial motte (cleared in 1936 to make way for a 'bus station) and a bailey running down the slope to the river's edge. Whatever was placed there by William's builders had been rebuilt a hundred years later, and the fragments which survive above ground or which have recently been excavated show still later stone buildings built within the castle walls.

The castle acted as a garrison point and a final place of refuge in troublesome times. But it was not long before the town itself received defences. Walls around the borough north of the Welland were probably in existence by the 1180s, and perhaps as early as the 1150s, to judge by the story of the siege of Stamford in 1153 when it took the Count of Anjou three assaults to capture the place. The walls were apparently often rebuilt, until in their final form they were made of stone, thick and strong, with a sentry-walk along the interior and fortified with a number of round bastions (one of which survives, though much mutilated) and with a wide ditch around the outside. At each of the main entrances, strong gates were built, most of them with rooms incorporated into them.

Parts of the town, however, still lay outside the walls. To the south, over the bridge, lay Stamford Without (later Stamford Baron). Basically, it consisted of houses and shops along the east-west Water Street and the main road to the south, but there were also a few side streets. Much of this suburb came into the possession of the Abbot of Peterborough and throughout the Middle Ages there was some uncertainty as to whether it formed part of Stamford or whether it fell into one of the neighbouring counties; at times, it was even taxed with rural Lincolnshire, to the north of the river. There were other suburbs outside the town walls. To the east, houses were built between St George's Gate and East Gate; along the road to the north (Scotgate now, *Scoftegate* then) lay the suburb of St Clements, while there may have been some housing outside the west gate of the town too, in the parish of St Mary Bynwerk (near the site of the later bastion).

The spread of these suburbs probably indicates the growth of the town, both in size and in wealth. It was still a small town by today's standards — probably only 5,000 or 6,000 at the height of its glory in the late thirteenth century. But this made for a major provincial town in the early Middle Ages. It housed substantial stone residences, some of them dating from the early years of the twelfth century, fragments of which survive, and in the thirteenth century, at the height of its glory, the halls built in the town for rich merchants, many with vaulted undercrofts, were as fine as those in any town in the realm without exception. The cellars in St Mary's Hill or in High Street, the arcaded great halls in St Paul's Street and elsewhere bear testimony to the wealth of the greatest residents of the town, as well as to the poverty in later centuries which prevented their replacement.

Each of the suburbs had its own parish church. St Mary Bynwerk (within the walls), originally St Mary *extra burgum* (outside the borough), lay near the west gate; St Clement's church (now known to have stood inside the walls) covered the houses along Scotgate, while in the eastern suburb stood Holy Trinity church (later called St Stephens). Stamford Baron to the south had two parish churches: All Saints by the Water and St Martin's.

But these were the surburban churches of Stamford. Within the mediaeval walls stood no less than nine more parish churches. Some were probably small and have now vanished, like St Michael's in Cornstall close by St George's Gate, and St Andrew's, the exact site of which is lost. The architectural remains of the five which survive show these to have been substantial buildings — St George and St Mary by the bridge, both in their own squares, St John now on the corner of High Street, All Saints in the Market (perhaps the oldest of them all) at the hub of the mediaeval town, and St Paul's with its Norman work, no longer used as a parish church but as a school chapel, near the East Gate. St Peter's, another early church, was associated with the castle but only the site survives now, while

St Michael the Greater has been almost entirely rebuilt in the nineteenth century, a true High Street church (now sadly mutilated).

The parish churches, together with six non-parochial chapels in and around the town, served the daily religious needs of the laity; they acted as focal points for all sorts of business. To judge from the quality of the thirteenth century building in them (especially All Saints in the Market and the tower of St Mary's), they were carefully tended and elaborately adorned by the wealthy. But there were other religious bodies in or near Stamford. The oldest was the priory that Durham built just to the east of Stamford, in the town fields by the river. Dated by legend to 658, it was in fact founded after the Conquest, probably about 1088. Large buildings (some of which survive) and a small number of monks characterise the history of St Leonard's throughout the Middle Ages. It managed the property which Durham owned in the town (including a substantial area of houses constituted as a separate manor under the title of St Cuthbert's fee, and including the patronage of the two churches dedicated to St Mary) and in the rest of eastern England. A similar arrangement existed in Stamford Baron; there a nunnery (St Michael's) belonging to Peterborough Abbey was established in the 1150s, and through it the abbey managed its estates in Stamford, including the five churches which it owned. A smaller convent existed at Wothorpe but, when it fell on hard times, it was dissolved and the remaining nun was transferred to St Michael's nunnery. The only other full monastic institution immediately adjacent to the town was the priory of Newstead, which stood on the river Gwash, just on the borders of Stamford's lands, adjoining Uffington parish. This too was responsible for one of the parish churches, Holy Trinity, which belonged to Belvoir Priory, the mother house of Newstead.

Monasteries farther afield held the other churches of the town. St Fromond in Normandy was the furthest away; it held five of the churches but had some difficulty in dealing with them and in securing the profits which should have come to them. Crowland Abbey owned St Michael the Greater. Other religious houses had a presence in the town in other ways. Some, like the abbeys of Bourne and Thorney, had substantial holdings of rents and property, while several others owned smaller estates. A large number of the houses of mediaeval Stamford paid some form of rent, usually through a local bailiff, to one monastery or another throughout England, from Croxden in Staffordshire to Southwick in Hants.

It is not to be wondered at, then, that when the begging friars came to England in the first half of the thirteenth century, they came to Stamford in strength. While other towns (like Leicester and Chester) as large or even larger than Stamford provided houses for two or three of the mendicant orders — indeed the major port of Southampton had only one house of friars — all four mendicant orders settled at Stamford. They went outside the walls for their sites, and built in style. The White friars and the Grey friars settled beyond the East Gate, knocking down houses as their buildings expanded. The Black friars built nearer the river, between St Leonard's priory and St George's Gate. To the west, the Friars of the Sack came and, when they were dissolved, after a short period when a Royal servant lived in the house in style, it was reconstituted as a house of Austin friars. The Stamford houses of friars soon became large and important centres in their respective orders.

While it may well have been trade which made these monasteries and friaries so interested in Stamford, their presence probably strengthened the existence of a number of schools there. These were certainly in existence by 1298 and probably earlier. Where they were held in the town is not clear but at least one (the Carmelite school) seems to have been located in St George's Square and another (Sempringham School) in St Peter's Street. Some of these had a high reputation; both Durham priory and the Gilbertine houses are known to have sent students to reside in their property in the town. Sempringham Hall, the school for the Gilbertines, is well recorded. It was established early in the fourteenth century by Robert Luterell of Irnham, who gave his house on the north side of St Peter's Street (then called 'the Gannoc') to Sempringham Abbey for students of the Gilbertine order. The mediaeval house, with its courtyard and its own chapel of St Mary, has now largely gone, but it is most likely that, apart from the half-dozen or so Gilbertine novices who lived there, other students resident in the town attended the school. At least two of the friaries also had notable schools in Stamford, known throughout the realm.

It may have been the presence of these schools which encouraged the northern students of Oxford when, disgruntled with their southern masters, they decided to secede, to set up a new University at first at Northampton and eventually in Stamford. This they did in 1334. Oxford clearly regarded this as a threat and petitioned the King, the Queen and the Bishop of Lincoln for its closure.

'Since, lady, certain persons who have obtained all their degrees from us, have now gone to Stamford, to the destruction . . . of our university, and are every day attracting others there by their false pretences',

the Oxford staff wrote to the Queen, begging her to intervene; this

'new assembly of scholars at the town of Stamford for University instruction', which is 'in every way hurtful and pestilential . . . we beg and beseech you (in this case, the king) to extirpate by your royal power, so that what was begun by improvident rashness may be quickly put an end to by the royal wisdom, and be a warning to future evil-doers'.

'Extirpated' it was, by Royal decree, despite a counter-petition (apparently supported by Peterborough Abbey) from 'the clerks living in the town of Stamford'. The only later evidences of it were an oath which all Oxford undergraduates until 1854 had to swear . . . 'that you will not lecture or attend lectures at Stamford, as in a university or general school or college', and a house in the town called Brazenose, the gate of which was said to be decorated with the original knocker from Brazenose Hall in Oxford; in order to recover this item of furniture the college bought the house in the late nineteenth century and took the knocker in triumph back to Oxford, leaving a replica in its place.

It was a short-lived but significant episode in the town's history, and one which the town has long cherished. Francis Peck called his *Annals of Stamford* in 1727 *Academia Tertia Anglicana:* 'England's third university'. Much was made of it in 1962 when the corporation was applying for one of the new universities then being set up. For it appeals to Stamford's character — academic and clerical: it was 'a place to study and become proficient in greater quiet and peace by sufferance of the noble John Earl of Warenne', in contrast with the more worldly Oxford with its 'many controversies, contests, and fights . . . by which great damages, dangers, deaths, murders, maimings and robberies have happened', as the students' petition put it.

Apart from the churches, monasteries and schools, the clerical character of mediaeval Stamford was strengthened by its hospitals, those small houses run by religious persons for the benefit of the old, the sick, the homeless and travellers. None of these was as important or as wealthy as St Leonard's in York or St Mark's in Bristol, but there were several smaller ones. There seem to have been two leper hospitals, one guarding the town on the south side and the other just to the east of the town, to house those poor afflicted wanderers, away from the burgesses and other residents. There were also two hospitals for pilgrims, again one in the eastern quarter of the town and the other to the south, though it seems that they ceased to exist after the middle of the thirteenth century. The most important of them all was a double hospital, that of St John the Baptist and St Thomas the Martyr. Part of the responsibility of this foundation was to maintain the town bridge (it was built over the bridge) and part was to care for the poor. It seems to have been linked with the gild of 'palmers' (ie those who had been to the Holy Land) when it was first established.

This emphasis on pilgrims reminds us that Stamford was a great place for passing through, in the Middle Ages as now. It lay on one of the main routes of mediaeval England. At first, this was the road from East Anglia to the North Midlands, Leicester, Nottingham and Newark. Later, from the 1170s, it stood on the road from London to York and the north. Before that date travellers from the south to the north, who wished to avoid a ferry crossing of either the Trent or the Humber, journeyed via Nottingham (where a York Street even today hints at this early road); those who travelled through Stamford were either going into or out of Lincolnshire (with its regional capital at Lincoln) or were passing from East Anglia to join the north-bound route. But in the second half of the twelfth century, a bridge was built over the Trent at Newark, and more and more traffic swung further east, to pass on its way from London through Stamford and Grantham to York and Scotland.

Thus it was that all the great and many of the lesser folk passed through the town some time during the Middle Ages. Pilgrims, travelling salesmen and Royal messengers; bishops on their visitations, great lords on their way to attend the King's person, lesser mortals to contest in the King's courts, foreign merchants scouring the land for wool, cloth and other produce, itinerant preachers, soldiers hastening (or otherwise) to the muster, bands of builders and entertainers — mediaeval Stamford saw all of these. Above all the King came, not just once but several times: Edward I is said to have paid no less than nine visits to the town in thirty years, on average one every three and a half years; and when the body of his dearly-loved wife was carried in style from Harby where she died to London, one of those famous Eleanor crosses was built in Scotgate, outside the northern gate, to mark the occasion. With their large numbers of attendants, such passages may have provided some opportunities for trading, but they must also have proved a burden on the borough's entertainment account.

Sometimes, the great came to stay for a time. Royal councils and later parliaments were summoned to meet in the town. On these occasions the King stopped at St Leonards or in one of the friaries around the town, while the nobles hired residence where they could: Stamford was already well-endowed with inns. And it went further than this: the religious orders held their provincial councils in Stamford on several occasions — even the White Canons, who had no house nearer to the town than Vaudey (now in Grimsthorpe Park) in Lincolnshire or Pipewell in Northamptonshire. Stamford had become something of a conference centre.

But some met at Stamford for less worthy purposes, and the traffic through the town meant that the inhabitants could not remain uninvolved in the troubles of these centuries. The borough was defended for Stephen during that troubled reign and was besieged three times, on the third occasion falling to the besiegers because the King was too busy investing Ipswich Castle to come to the aid of the defenders; thus Henry Duke of Normandy (the future Henry II) marched on from Stamford to Nottingham. And later, in the reigns of John and his son Henry III, Stamford was frequently the centre of the muster of rebellious nobles and their troops. One reason for this was that the town was a centre for legitimate tournaments, which the King licensed over a wide area of England, stretching from Oxford bridge to the bridge at Stamford. Under cover of these mediaeval equivalents of the modern horse trials, groups of dissident nobles met and plotted, as frequent Royal prohibitions clearly reveal.

Stamford thus was perforce within the main stream of English politics during the twelfth and thirteenth centuries. And as such, the King began to treat it as a piece of private property. Henry II, having won it by force, gave it to a friend and loyal supporter, the Norman Richard de Humet, King's Constable and Sheriff of Rutland; it is this overlordship which probably accounts for the interests of at least two Normandy monasteries in the town. During John's reign, the Norman lords were dispossessed and the King gave the town to his cousin, William de Warenne, who had lost his French lands. When William died (in 1240), Henry III first kept the town in his own hands, then gave it to his son prince Edward, who later gave it back to the Warenne family. All of Stamford's lords were then closely related to the King himself.

These men did not live in Stamford, though they may have visited it on occasion. Rather, they managed their courts and collected their tolls, taxes and fines by bailiffs and stewards. And this gave the inhabitants of Stamford an opportunity to secure some control over their own affairs — though at times their view of their privileges and the view of their lords' officials did not always tally. Well before 1200 (or so the town alleged) the people of Stamford controlled their own local taxes and received certain tolls in support of some of the town's hospitals; indeed, as early as 1086, the town was divided into six 'wards', presumably with two laymen each forming some kind of a common council. In 1202, King John confirmed the 'ancient customs' of the borough. Most of the inhabitants' interests were directed towards trade. In 1257, the burgesses were allowed to unite into a closed shop (a 'commune'), though this was probably short-lived; and in 1313, Warenne surrendered to the burgesses the tolls in the market and sanctioned the annual election of a chief officer for the town, though he reserved the right to approve the election. Thereafter, late in September every year, an 'alderman' was chosen and shortly afterwards presented to the lord's steward in Stamford Castle to take his oath.

Trade was the main interest of these men, and it was on trade that Stamford's greatness was built. Primarily, Stamford was a market town. It stood between great agricultural regions, and thus exchanged wool and meat from the grazing areas for corn and iron products from the arable areas and the forest smelters. Throughout the town stood markets — the 'white meat' market in what is now Red Lion Square, the flesh-market or shambles in front of St Michael's church, the beast market in Broad Street and sheep market in Red Lion Square. Around the market cross and its well were the sellers of butter and eggs; the corn market stood inside St George's Gate in Cornstall. And those who did not rent a stall in one of these market places sold from baskets or from their shop windows — even in Stamford Baron. Early market charters for the town do not exist; the rights are probably of such antiquity as to have been prescriptive. The rich lands around Stamford — the fens developed by the monasteries and a large population of independent farmers, the forest areas and the limestone uplands with their sheep-walks — poured their wealth every Friday into Stamford, to be dispersed to others who came to buy.

Some of this produce, of course, stayed in Stamford: the wool, for instance. There is some evidence for woollen cloth being made and/or finished in Stamford — more perhaps being finished, dyed and cut and made up than woven there. Relatively few weavers occur in the records, and no examples of weavers' houses survive, though a few loom weights have been found in excavations in the town. But dyers and tailors are frequently mentioned. Some of their houses survive, with cellar-type workhouses-cum-shops below the street level, their entrance steps forming a danger to all passing traffic, and living rooms above. Elsewhere throughout the town, men built pottery kilns (until the middle of the thirteenth century when the local industry apparently died out), tanning vats and perhaps iron-smelting furnaces. The tenter meadows near the river were leased out by the town council later in the Middle Ages. But for all this industry, Stamford remained close to the soil. It had extensive open fields around its wall, and farming was a common occupation of its residents. Herds of cows, flocks of sheep and other farm stock must have been a daily sight in the streets of mediaeval Stamford; the council regularly tried to limit the accumulation of animal manure at the doors of the town's farmhouses within the walls.

All of which was a nuisance on market day; but more so at the time of the mid-Lent fair. Today the roundabouts and stalls stay for five days and block all the main streets of the town; during the Middle Ages, the fair lasted for two or three weeks and was a trading occasion of some importance to the nation as a whole. The King sent his servants to Stamford fair to buy the green and scarlet cloth for himself, his Queen and his household or to give as presents to other kings or visiting dignitaries. Foreign luxury goods and other supplies were purchased there for the court and for parliament. The nobles and monasteries replenished their stocks and bought the newest fashions; merchants from abroad, doing the rounds of England's great marts, always fitted in a visit to Stamford fair — in 1227, the King ordered the fair bailiffs to arrest all unlicensed French merchants who attended the fair.

A great national event, then, was under way in Stamford during Lent. Merchants from neighbouring towns like Leicester rented shops at their common expense and collected their own tolls on the goods sold. The Leicester merchants who visited the fair were told by their town council to 'place their mechandise where they had been accustomed to do, the clothiers on the southern, the wool-dealers on the northern part'. The merchandise was as multifarious as the buyers and sellers; and much of the produce was exported through the ports of the Wash by alien merchants.

And some of these alien merchants stayed in the town. It was a convenient centre for trading on a more permanent basis than the annual fair. Mostly they were wool and cloth merchants — men like Eustace Malherbe and Terricus of Cologne, who bought property in and around the town and exported large stocks of wool through Boston and King's Lynn. The Flemings were there too, Walter le Fleming and his relatives. So were Norman and Lombard merchants, especially the Florentines. They played their full part in the town, for its well-being was in their interest. They often managed its finances, especially the tax which was collected to keep the town walls in repairs.

Above all, there were the Jews. Stamford had a large number of Jews resident in the town — not as many nor as wealthy as those in Lincoln but more than Cambridge had. They were of course unpopular, perhaps as much for their money-lending as for their trade or their religious practices; incidents involving violence occurred in Stamford as in other places frequently, in 1189, 1223 and again in 1242. At times the Jews had to flee to the castle for protection, and on one occasion their synagogue was burnt. But they stayed until they were forced out of the realm in 1290; and their importance in the mediaeval economy of Stamford can be seen in that after they went, Stamford was never the same.

Norman arches and buttress near bridge, beneath Burghley's hospital
in flood.

The castle; ABOVE: drawing by Stukeley; (SLHS) CENTRE: from thirteenth century hall; BELOW: exterior view of hall.

Town defences; ABOVE: the sole surviving bastion; BELOW: St George's gate, from interior.

ABOVE: St Leonard's Priory, late twelfth century; LEFT: St Mary's church: tower of thirteenth century (spire is later); RIGHT: detail of High Street, St Martin's undercroft.

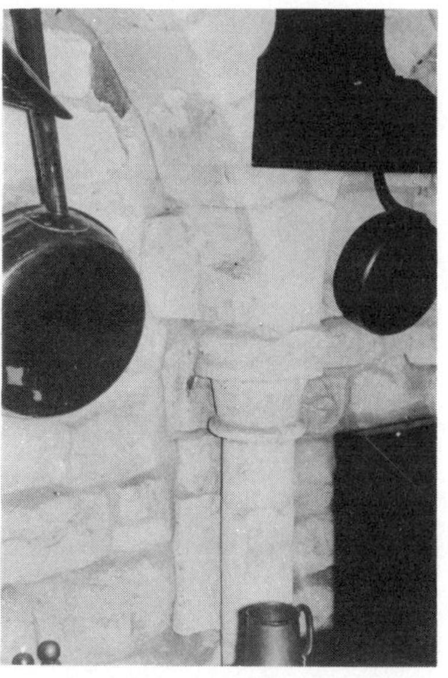

LEFT: Undercrofts: ABOVE; St Mary's Hill; CENTRE: High Street. BELOW: High Street, St Martin's. RIGHT: Examples of fragments of thirteenth century hall houses. ABOVE: St Mary's Hill. BELOW: St Paul's Street (this house has now been completely reconstructed).

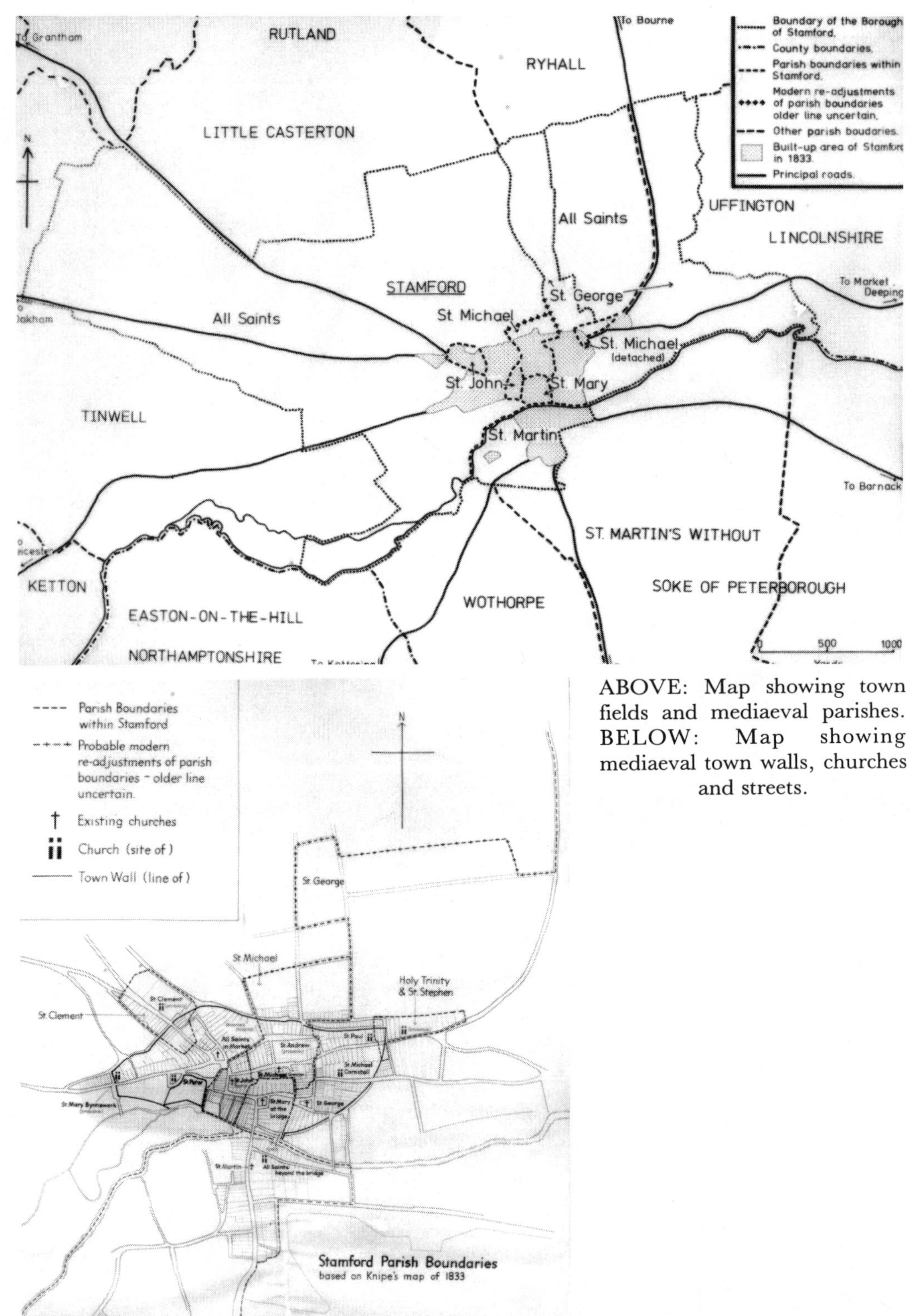

ABOVE: Map showing town fields and mediaeval parishes. BELOW: Map showing mediaeval town walls, churches and streets.

Fluctuating Fortunes, 1300-1550

Richard Butcher, 1646

In 1340, the King's commissioners descended once more on Stamford, to inquire into the state of the Royal castle there. They reported:

'The castle is old and the walls decayed; within are an old tower, a great hall, a chamber with solar [a sort of private withdrawing room], a chapel, a turret and a house for a prison, all of no value'.

It was neglect rather than military action which had brought the castle to this sorry state. It was no longer important to the King, and his noble subjects the Warennes, who had held it for most of the thirteenth century, had concentrated more on other parts of their far-flung estates in East Anglia, or in Grantham twenty-four miles or so to the north. It is a paradox that when Stamford came into the possession of members of the Royal family (the Lord Edward, son of Henry III, or the Earls of Northampton under Edward III) it became of still less importance, a source of income rather than a place of residence. Certainly few efforts seem to have been made to restore the castle to its former glory, as recent excavations have shown.

What was true of the castle seems to have been true of the town as a whole. From about 1300 or even earlier, Stamford entered into a period of decline, from which it did not entirely recover for more than three hundred years. There was a temporary and minor improvement in the second half of the fifteenth century, with substantial achievements; but behind this lay real problems, and the sixteenth century saw still further setbacks.

It seems to have started in the late thirteenth century. The expulsion of the Jews affected trade, as did the wars with France and the accompanying export restrictions which followed. The decline of the wool trades was not fully compensated in Stamford's case by the rise of cloth exports. It is true that Stamford was for a time designated in 1353 as one of a number of 'staple' towns for the sale and export of wool, but this short-lived experiment merely added to uncertainties, instead of providing a real basis for prosperity. It is not long before we begin to read of property in the centre of the town being in ruins — and staying in ruins for a long time. Edward III's erratic treatment of rich alien merchants in an attempt to use them to finance his French wars undermined business confidence further. The efforts in the 1330s of the northern students to establish a new university in the town was a 'last fling' and was in any case soon stifled by command of bishop and king.

Then came the Black Death. While we cannot know how many people in Stamford died of the plague in 1349 and in the severe later outbreak in 1361 (the Second Pestilence which especially hit children) and in the Third Pestilence of 1375, we can be sure the figure was substantial. Most of the suburbs declined. The parish and the church of St Michael Cornstall (clustered around St George's Gate) vanished early in the fourteenth century; St Mary Bynwerk at the opposite end of the town (just inside the bastion) probably ceased at the time of the plague, while the parishioners of Holy Trinity (in the eastern suburb between St Paul's Gate and the Greyfriars) and St Clement (the parish of which covered Scotgate suburb and was described in 1361 as 'much reduced because of the plague') both had to resort to special measures to support their parish clergy. Early in the next century, the parishioners of All Saints by the Water, south of the Welland, gave up the struggle to keep their church going and joined with St Martin's.

Only the four great friaries seem to have been exempt from this general decline. Still lavishly patronised by many of the greatest of noble families in the realm, including Richard II's mother (Joan of Kent) and the Earl of Lancaster's daughter, Blanche Lady Wake, these buildings were being adorned and endowed to house the tombs of the wealthy, while the King on occasion resided and held court in the friaries, and national ecclesiastical councils continued to be held there. The Greyfriars had a new gatehouse built in the fourteenth century (now mis-called the White friars); the glory of the Whitefriars was testified to by several later writers, while the Blackfriars, after the Dissolution, became a coveted piece of property for several successive gentle families. Even the Austin friary to the west, after a hesitant start, apparently achieved considerable wealth and adornment, to judge by the fragments known to have come from the site in later years.

Almost all of this fine creation of the fourteenth century has now vanished. What little building work survives from these years is poorer in quality than that of the previous and succeeding centuries. When St George's church was reconstructed during the fourteenth century, the building was patched up with indifferent workmanship, as if both money and skills were in short supply, in sharp contrast with the fine work of the previous century. Again the fourteenth century vicarage house of St Mary's parish (in St Mary's street) is plain, and contrasts with All Saints vicarage (at the bottom of Barn Hill) built in the following century.

But above all, there seems to have been a major decline in the great fair of Stamford. Less is heard of it in the fourteenth than in the thirteenth century. Probably the Hundred Years War against France (which began in 1337) prevented the alien merchants from attending in large numbers. But there was also a decline both in the wool trade and in the cloth industry in the Stamford region. Throughout the century the ports of the Wash and East Coast show signs of suffering — from war and piracy, from silting and from changes in the patterns of trade. Exports of wool to foreign parts fell substantially during the fourteenth century, and what was exported seems to have been bought directly from the producers, thus by-passing the fairs. And there was a decline also in the demand for the traditional cloths of Lincoln and Stamford. New centres of cloth-making emerged, in East Anglia, in the Cotswolds and in the West Riding of Yorkshire. It is significant that when, in 1401, the King sent purchasers to Stamford fair for his household, it was to buy horses, not cloth.

There seems to have been something of a recovery in the fifteenth century. It is hard to be certain of this. Certainly there were some wealthy merchants in the town, of whom William Browne, Calais stapler — called by Leland 'a merchant of a very wonderfulle bigness' — was the most outstanding. He was a wool merchant who clearly ran a large multiple company with his brother John and nephew (and eventual successor) Christopher; but it is significant that Christopher moved out of Stamford to London when he succeeded to the headship of the firm. That London instead of the East Coast ports became the focus of the town's economic activity meant that the major arteries of trade came into fewer hands; it was the growth of London's hold over the country's economy which made towns like Stamford concentrate more and more on local rather than international trade.

Most of the other wealthy inhabitants of Stamford operated on a more localised basis than the Brownes. Sir William Bruges, it is true, became Garter King of Arms and his will provided new windows for St George's church in the 1450s. But more typical was William Hykeham, a baker who helped to rebuild the north chapel in St Mary's church, apparently used by the Corpus Christi gild.

This was one of the many building projects in Stamford then; most of the town's surviving parish churches were substantially reconstructed or beautified between 1450 and 1500. The external walls of All Saints in the Market were pulled down to window-sill level, and the church was rebuilt with new windows and a new tower, mostly by the Browne family, to judge by the merchant's marks still to be found on the building. St John's church received a new roof and new glass by a number of patrons in or about 1451. And William Browne used his great wealth — and his lack of a male heir — to found in 1475 a wealthy and ornate hospital for old people, a hospital which survived the disasters of the Reformation and the legal wrangles of the nineteenth century to become (as some think) the inspiration of Trollope's novel *The Warden,* and to remain one of Stamford's most beautiful of buildings, with its fine details and rich glass.

Ecclesiastical building was matched by houses. It is probable that the fine jettied building along the south side of Red Lion Square, lying behind a Georgian facade but still with substantial fragments of a great fifteenth century roof, is the remains of the Browne family's Woolhouse. All Saints Vicarage is amongst the last of the stone buildings, although an undercroft in St Mary's Place shows that others were built on an elaborate scale. More typical is the timber-framed style of the Vaults and 43-44 St Mary's Street, a style fully developed as the sixteenth century progressed. Deeds shows a good deal of rebuilding at this time on a larger scale than earlier.

But if there were the builders, the successful merchants, the Brownes and the Hykehams, there were also the Kestevens. Thomas Kesteven, like Browne, was a town councillor and Calais Stapler; but for him life was hard. He was a member of the famous firm of wool dealers, the Celys, and acted as their agent in Calais while at the same time trading in his own behalf. His house in Calais, with its woolstore, was one of the main centres of distribution for the Cely trade on the continent. But Kesteven fell out with his wealthy patrons; he incurred heavy debts and was unable to pay them. In 1479 he was forced to write: 'I have removed and taken me a lesser lodging . . . In my little lodging that I am now in I have a fair stable and a fair room and a chamber for all my good masters and friends, if it please any of them to see me in my poverty — a little further from the market it is'. Eventually in 1482, he wrote from Calais in despair: 'I must continue here all my life, the which is to my sore trial . . .' To comfort him on his 'low days', he took to philosophy: 'I am not alone in sorrow — I see daily kings, princes and other estates from the highest to the lowest brought down, now high, now rich, now poor, now alive, now dead. He that has his life and has nothing, that previously had riches, is worst at ease'. Thomas Kesteven presents to us another face of early capitalism in Stamford, the merchant who did not quite make it.

Perhaps it was this uncertainty that parallelled the rebuilding of some of the many parish churches of Stamford with the decline of others. We know less of these, because most of them no longer survive; but what evidence there is does not suggest that much in the way of beautification was done in the churches of Holy Trinity, St Clement's, St Peter's, St Michael's the Greater, St Paul's or in the lost St Andrew's. Holy Trinity probably ceased for a time, and when its parishioners (less than ten persons lived in the parish, according to an inquiry in 1428) got it going again by forming a gild to support the incumbent who was 'very poor', it was called the parish church of St Stephen. Similarly, a chantry (or private mass priest) was established in St Clement's church and soon this became more important than the parish work; the incumbent was appointed by the town's alderman and not by the original patron of the church.

This is one example of the growth of gilds and chantries in Stamford between about 1300 and 1500. St Mary's gild was the oldest and the wealthiest; it met in St Mary's church, as did the gild of Corpus Christi which emerged at about the time of the Black Death. Most of the other parish churches had their gilds, like St Martin's which, as early as 1389, was responsible for a town bull (later it became associated with bull-running in the town). St Katherine's gild met in the room over the porch of St Paul's church and seems to have survived as long as the parish did, until the end of the fifteenth century.

Fourteen parishes were, by 1515, reduced to ten. It is alleged in most of the Stamford histories that these churches were destroyed in the sack of the town by the Lancastrian army in 1461. But this 'sack' has perhaps been over-estimated by the local historians. Henry VI, the 'saintly king', had been defeated by Richard, Duke of York, who pursued the remnants of the Lancastrian army into the north, only to be defeated in his turn and killed. Queen Margaret, Henry's French consort, rallied her supporters and marched south, sacking Yorkist centres of support on the way — and so it was that Stamford suffered. How much destruction was actually done in the town by 'the misruled and outrageous people in the north parties of this realm' who (so it is alleged by the loyalist propaganda machine)

'by the way compelled, despoiled, robbed and destroyed all manner of chattel, victual and riches',

'robbing all the country and people as they came, and spoiling abbeys and houses of religion and churches and bore away chalices, books and other ornaments, as they had been pagans or Saracens and no Christian men' (as later chronicles put it),

is not clear; as with so much in the fifteenth century, the evidence is contradictory. On the one hand, Leland as late as the 1540s speaks of the sack (which he attributes to the reign of one of the first three Edwards, ie 1272-1377) and says that the town is 'not synce fully re-edified'; on the other hand, as we have seen, most of the 'lost' churches had vanished before 1461, and the architectural evidence that remains suggests that more survived than we might have supposed from such a 'sack' — glass in the windows of St John's and St George's churches, for instance, and even Yorkist symbols in St Mary's church windows. One church was rebuilt after the sack, St Martin's in Stamford Baron under the patronage of the Bishop of Lincoln, John Russell, in the 1480s; but the long gap between the 'sack' and the rebuilding of what was by then the only parish church south of the river argues against extensive damage having been done twenty or more years earlier. The borough records start in 1465 and earlier records are missing ('The northern men . . . brennid many writings of their antiquities and privileges', according to Leland) — but some of these records survived into the early seventeenth century and even later rather than being burnt in the 'sack'. In any case, other towns on the route, like Grantham and Huntingdon, were also 'sacked' by the same army, but they do not claim any permanent significance for that event in the way Stamford does — the 'sack' is part of Stamford's mythology, created by the town's early antiquarian tendencies.

Nevertheless, 'sacked' the town was, whatever that implied. And with reason, too. Stamford was after all owned by successive Dukes of York (to whom it had passed in 1363), and it had twice before given the Lancastrian administration cause for concern in the 1450s in support for its overlord; indeed in 1452, along with Grantham, it was the centre of a serious rising against the government. Later, in 1470, when the Dukes of York had become Kings of England, Edward IV was grateful once more for its loyalty, for when the Lincolnshire Lords Welles and Willoughby rose against his rule, the two armies met outside Stamford and fought an engagement, in which the rebels were so overwhelmed that they shed their coats in their anxiety to run away: the battle of Loosecoat Field.

And the town was rewarded for its loyalty. Less than a year after coming to the throne, Edward IV granted to the town its great charter of incorporation (1462). It had already, as we have seen, received from earlier lords — notably the Warennes — earlier charters, granting it privileges which usually graced a major town; but now came the major accolade, incorporate status. Some towns like Bristol had received this earlier, it is true; others were to wait longer — until they could secure the right sort of patronage. Stamford's turn came early in 1462.

The rewards were substantial: two persons elected to represent the newly created corporation in parliament; a town bench of JPs and a bailiff to execute the King's writs instead of the Sheriff. A borough council was set up under the Alderman; there was a First Twelve (Capital Burgesses) and a Second Twelve (Comburgesses) with the rest of the Freemen meeting once a year for the elections. And although the King's steward (or his deputy) was still a figure to be reckoned with or to be placated with grants of wine and the like, the council settled down to run the town and improve its fortunes.

How successful they were we cannot be sure. In 1481, towards the end of Edward IV's reign, they obtained a second charter from the King in which financial considerations were more to the fore: a new weekly market and two new fairs at Corpus-Christi-tide and at the feast of SS Simon and Jude, and an endowment of property to the corporation to maintain the town walls. But this may be a sign of growing impoverishment rather than better fortunes.

It is not at all clear how the town was faring in the last decades of the Middle Ages. There were wealthy merchants (especially wool merchants) in Stamford at the end of the fifteenth century; but the economic basis of the town was more mixed than in earlier periods. A review of the freemen of the borough in this period provides some indicators. In order to exercise their trade or craft in Stamford, all persons had to apply to the borough council to be 'made free of the town'; on payment of a fine (remitted if they had been born in Stamford) and on finding suitable pledges, they were admitted to 'scot and lot' and thus could trade and vote in burgess elections and were responsible to pay to the borough rates.

Lists of freemen, usually with their occupations given, survive in the Hall Books of the town. A full analysis cannot be given here, but some general points can be made. First, it is clear that not all economic activities are recorded; some whole groups are omitted and presumably were able to trade without becoming freemen. Secondly, a number of persons listed have no occupation given — out of 1,365 recorded admissions in the first hundred years of the surviving records, 1465-1565, 75 (just over 5%) had no occupations recorded (most of them in the first few years of the borough records). It is, I think, unreasonable to assume that these 75 should be equally distributed throughout the occupational categories. It is surely more likely that it was customary for certain groups of people to be admitted without recording their occupations. These persons thus have been omitted from the analysis which follows.

We know then the occupation or status of some 1,290 new freemen. Of these, there were three main groupings. The largest (22%) was engaged in the textile industries and trade. Mercers and drapers formed just under a quarter, industrial processes (weavers, dyers, fullers and the like) rather more than a quarter of this group. Almost exactly a half of all textile workers were those who processed the cloth, ranging from tailors and haberdashers to pointmakers and broderers. The second major category (19%) was the group of leather workers, of whom a sixth were tanners and others engaged in initial processes, more than a third were shoemakers, a similar number were engaged in other leather industries (glovers, saddlers, etc) and the remainder were in associated industries (such as tallow chandlers). The third main group (21.4%) went under the uncertain term of labourer.

After these three, there was only one large group of trades, the victuallers (12.6%). Some 8.0% were engaged in building, 5% in metal work of some kind or other (smiths, wrights, ironmongers and some locksmiths, pewterers and goldsmiths) and rather more than 3% in agriculture. What is significant is that 3½% were engaged in what might be called 'service trades' — surgeons, barbers, servants, minstrels, notaries and scriveners, cooks and carters. Although this is a small element, it is significant for the nature of the town.

Only 1.7% of all the named entries recorded social status, esquire, yeoman or gentleman — 22 out of 1,290 in all. Admission to the freedom of the borough for social reasons was apparently sparingly used, unless of course those not given any occupation fell within this class.

In other words, Stamford at the end of the Middle Ages was a town at the cross-roads; it could continue as a textile town or develop into a leatherworking town. Gentility and service elements were small but still significant.

What sort of a town was it then about 1500? It was not overcrowded, as some towns were. There were gardens and orchards, barns and farmyards and other open spaces inside the walls. Some of the streets (like Cheyne Lane with its early sixteenth century timber-framed houses which still survive) were narrow, and the wider ones were cluttered up with stalls, stone steps and manure heaps, those 'mucke hylls and donghills' which the new town council sought to regulate in 1466. There were still many stone houses, but most of the new building was being done in timber, of which only the largest and very best examples like the Cross Keys have survived. The rich were beginning to congregate in certain areas, especially All Saints parish; the suburbs were dying and the poorer lived down by the river and in St George's parish. Around the town stood the four great friaries, still large, privileged and beautiful. The stone of the church buildings was coming to contrast more and more sharply with the timber of the houses, especially as the castle was dismantled and the town walls in places were breached (despite the siege of 1461).

But the church was beginning to lose whatever hold on society it had had in Stamford, as elsewhere. The monasteries of St Michael's (with its constant scandals and its estates mismanaged) and Newstead were known to be in financial difficulties. Only a caretaker lived in St Leonard's. The friaries were standing more than half empty, increasingly anachronisms from an earlier age. The hospitals became impoverished and fell under lay control, until in 1548 the income of one of the biggest of them (St John and St Thomas) was being used to send the son of John Stodard, a leading burgess, to university at Cambridge, 'towards his exhibicion at Schole'. Everywhere, lay influence was growing; most of the parish churches had passed from ecclesiastical into lay patronage by the beginning of the sixteenth century and, throughout the town, burgesses and others met and feasted in their parish gilds, attended the Corpus Christi pageants and looked after their poor, their young and their sick in their own way. It is not without significance that in the late fifteenth century there was a move to persuade the Bishop of Lincoln to allow all of the parish churches to celebrate their patronal grants on the same day in September — an unsuccessful attempt to establish a new civic festival which had economic as well as religious motives at its roots.

Whether dissent had grown in the town or not is unknown. The proximity of Stamford to Leicester, a major centre for the Lollards of the fifteenth century, may have led to some heresy in the town of which no record now survives. Nor, when the Reformation came, are there many signs of the new thinking. It is true that when a layman, a merchant called William Radcliffe, founded the town's first free grammar school in 1532, he linked it to St John's College, Cambridge, one of the centres of the new reform movement. A Dominican friar who preached in St Martin's church for the retention of orthodoxy was attacked by the congregation. But probably the major factor was not so much outright rebellion against the old religion as an atmosphere of neglect. A visitation of the churches in the 1470s noted that a number of them were in decay: St Martin's chancel was falling down and St Mary's chancel was 'ruinous'. Leland, writing in the 1530s, speaks of the glories of the town as lying in the past. Stamford in 1500 was already suffering acutely. It may be significant that no less than five charitable gilds and fraternities were founded in the town between 1506 and 1548; poverty called for measures of aid and self-help.

ABOVE: The so-called White Friars' Gate; LEFT: in the early nineteenth century; (SLHS) RIGHT: as now; BELOW: Brazenose Gate; RIGHT: St George's church, mainly fourteenth century, but tower is later.

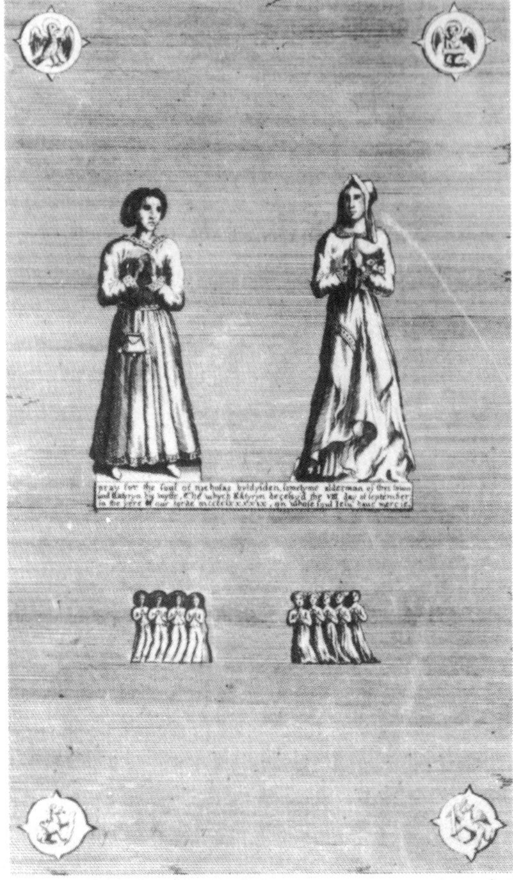

ABOVE: brasses; LEFT: Henry Wykys, vicar of All Saints and trustee for William Browne (1508), Stukeley drawing; (SLHS) RIGHT: Nicholas Byllysden, Alderman of Stamford, and wife (1499).

OPPOSITE: Fifteenth century churches with similar towers; ABOVE: St Martin's from the east; (BL) CENTRE: St John's church; RIGHT: nave roof, St John's church; BELOW: All Saints church, largely reconstructed in the fifteenth century by the wool-merchant family of Browne: view published in Peck and signed by Stukeley; (SLHS) RIGHT: porch.

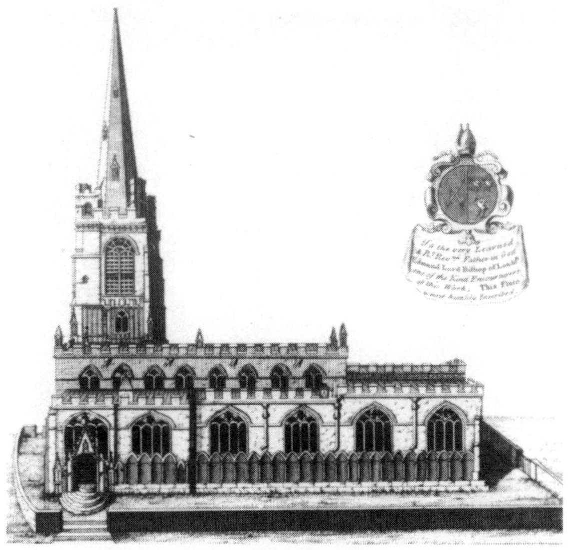

ABOVE LEFT: All Saints interior (note brasses on the wall to left); RIGHT: view from west; (BL) BELOW: the Browne family: brass of William and Agnes (1483).

ABOVE: Browne's Hospital, before restoration. BELOW: Audit Room
of Browne's Hospital.

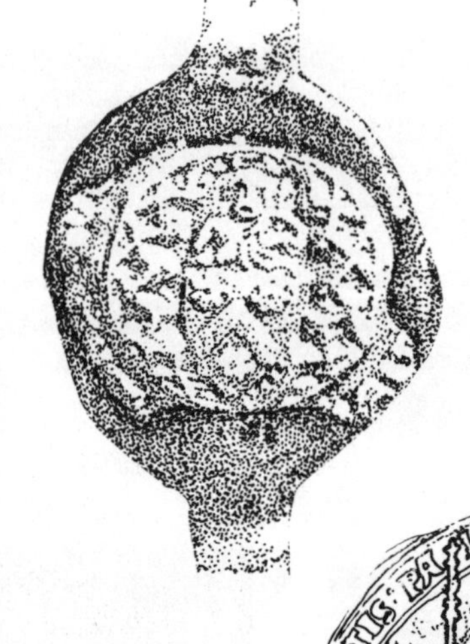

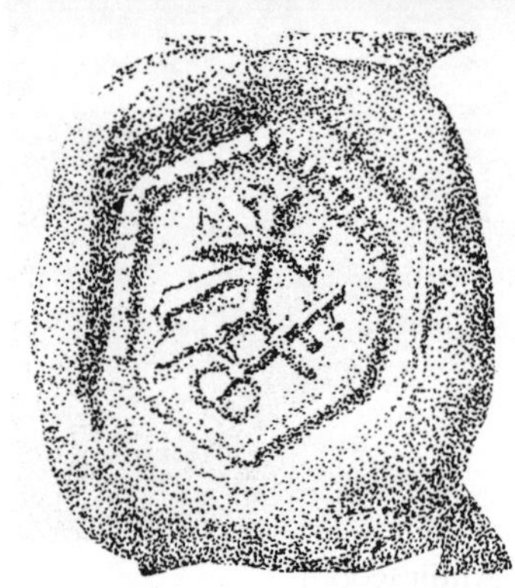

ABOVE LEFT: Portrait in window of Browne's Hospital (BL); RIGHT: fragments of a large mediaeval building survive in this shop off Red Lion Square, perhaps the Browne's 'Wool-Hall'. Seals of Stamford mediaeval residents; BELOW LEFT: a merchant; RIGHT: William, Earl Warenne. (DF: originals in PRO).

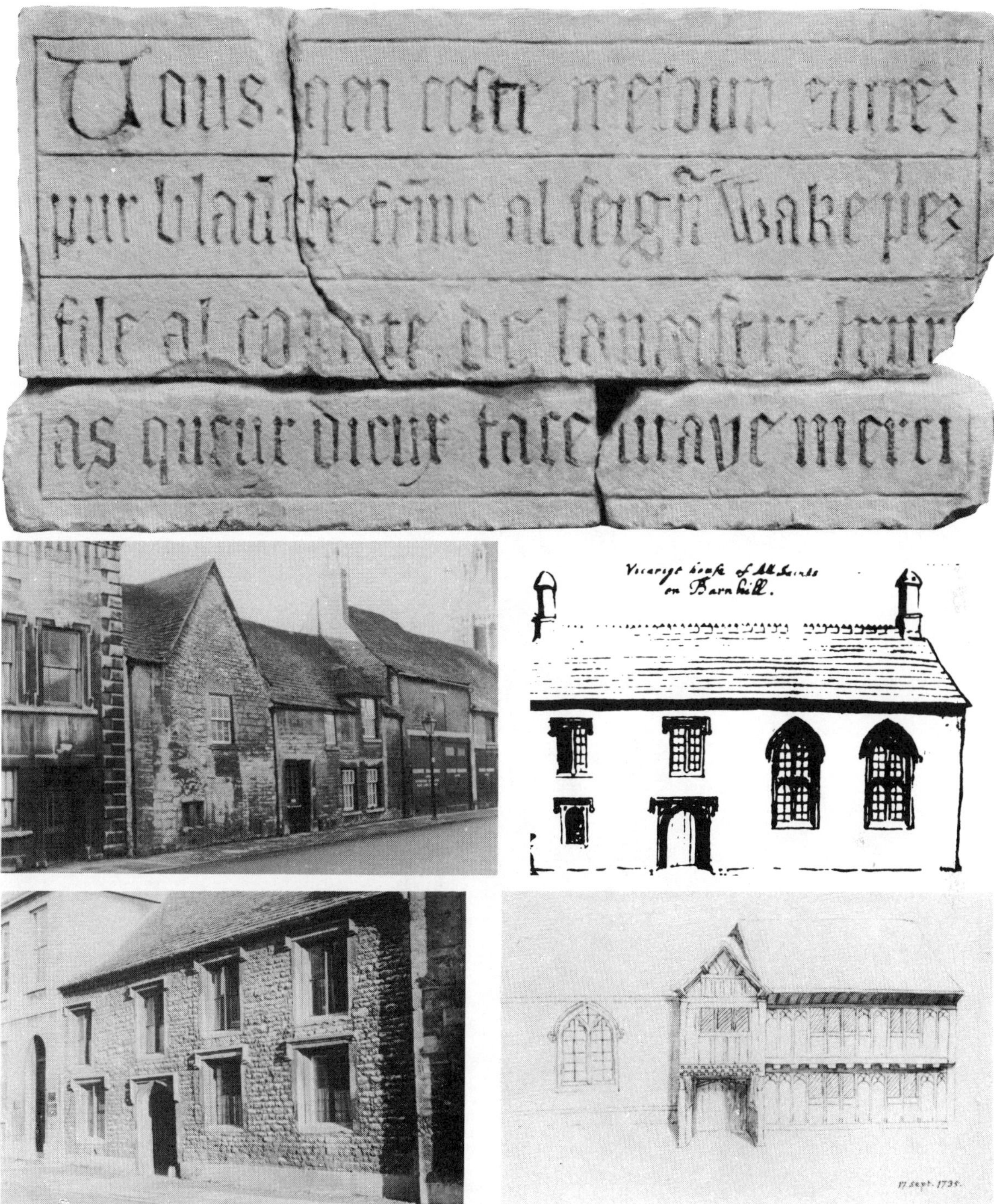

ABOVE: burial stone of Joan, Lady Wake, in Whitefriars. Mediaeval vicarages; CENTRE LEFT: St Mary's vicarage; RIGHT: All Saints vicarage, drawn by Stukeley, and BELOW LEFT: now; RIGHT: one of several large houses of late mediaeval date which Stukeley claimed were built for the 'university' of Stamford. (SLHS)

Drawing by Stukeley of effigy discovered in the town in 1731.

Years of Turbulence 1500-1660

While therefore, there is any thing of Gratitude
   left within our Walls,
It will always show it self in zeal for the Cecils;
   which Noble
Family me desire may Encrease, and Flourish, in
   accumulating
Wealth and Honours, till there shall arise a Greater
   Elizabeth, or a more justly Renown'd Lord-Treasurer.

Howgrave, 1726

The decline of the religious institutions of the town in the preceding one hundred or so years did not soften the effects on Stamford of the Reformation, when it came in the middle of the sixteenth century. Instead it ushered in a period of civic disturbances unprecedented and long-lasting. Stamford had not, of course, been immune from the general violence of mediaeval society, nor from the political upheavals of earlier years; in the twelfth and early thirteenth century it had formed a focal point for rebellion and had suffered musterings, sieges and capture on several occasions. Again in the fifteenth century, with armed conflict in the neighbourhood (and indeed on occasion in the streets of the town) in 1452, 1461 and 1470, the inhabitants knew the agonies of taking sides. But from the middle years of the sixteenth century to the Restoration, the town became the arena for the expression of divisions and conflicts among its own citizens; burgess fought against burgess; calling in when necessary outside help.

The upheavals of the Reformation seem to have started this process. The friaries, with their comings and goings and with their national and indeed international links, were closed; the three monasteries were dissolved and dismantled. Only one of these sites (Blackfriars) became a residence on a large scale, another (the nunnery of St Michael) a farmhouse. The rest were left as quarries for building stone. The parish churches became poorer, and the chantries and gilds, so carefully collected, vanished. Both the newly established grammar school and Browne's Hospital survived, it is true, but all the rest went. There must have been a greater sense of isolation from the outside world in the Stamford of 1550 as a result of these changes than ever before.

This upheaval was not achieved without some measure of religious dissension. 'Reformed' opinions were expressed vociferously and even violently in St Martin's church on at least one occasion, as we have seen, and Hugh Latimer preached in the cause of the Reformation in the town in 1550. The Pilgrimage of Grace and the Lincolnshire rising in the 1530s did not leave Stamford unscathed; the Duke of Suffolk mustered troops in the town in 1536 and took the surrender of the rebels here, and Henry VIII himself came in 1541. Several of the parishes were amalgamated in the 1540s by Act of Parliament or by other process, leaving the six (five north of the river, one south) which persisted for the next four hundred years. The introduction of Walloon Huguenot textile workers later in the century with their own 'Strangers' Church' and minister seems to have formed the first organised expression of puritanism. But none of this overcame Stamford's relative isolation, the smaller scale of its thinking, the reduction of the town to a regional marketing centre.

And this despite the meteoric rise to power of one of its own children. William Cecil, son and grandson of Stamford burgesses, obtained employment in the household of the young Princess Elizabeth and, after her accession, became her most trusted councillor. He did not forget his home town, for out of it he made his fortune — or perhaps it may be better to say that in it he invested his fortune. He, his relatives and friends, acquired estate after estate in the neighbourhood by gift, purchase, exchange or other means. The town even alleged that when they asked him in 1561 to secure for them the lordship of the manor of Stamford and all its rights from the Crown, he obtained it for himself, the year after he had obtained from Queen Elizabeth the lordship of the manor of Stamford Baron south of the river Welland. And so began that love-hate relationship which has been the theme of so much of Stamford's history from 1560 onwards. Perhaps it is a sign of Cecil's aloofness (so well betrayed in his letters to the town) that he built his great mansion in, and took his title from, the parish next to Stamford, Burley (or Burghley, as it came to be). Begun in the reign of Mary, Elizabeth's sister, it took many years to build and furnish, and formed one (but not apparently the most favourite) of Cecil's various residences.

Cecil came from a line of Stamford merchants and lawyers. He probably owed part of his advancement to the Protestant noble-lady Katherine, daughter of Lord Willoughby of Eresby of nearby Grimsthorpe; Katherine, a friend of Bishop Latimer, married Henry VIII's favourite, Charles Brandon, Duke of Suffolk and resided in the family house in Stamford, in which she was ordered for a time to entertain Mary Queen of Scots when she fled to England. Cecil carried on this tradition of loyalty to the 'reformed faith' and service to the Crown. Stamford saw much coming and going from such links with the court in Westminster.

Conflict and co-operation between the town and its new lord started at once. On the one hand, Cecil agreed to his nomination to the post of Recorder of the town, and his patronage was gratefully accepted by the burgesses until, in the 1620s, the Cecil interests in Stamford passed by marriage to the Derbyshire family of Lord Grey of Groby, who from 1628 were known as Earls of Stamford (although the Greys did not become legally lords of the manor of Stamford until 1640, it is clear that they were running the town well before this date). There was benefit from such direct patronage in the form of facilities for the town — a new town hall in 1558 and later a gaol, both provided by the Cecils, together with new conduits and the rebuilding of the bridge in 1570 after the old one was swept away in a flood (although the town council still had to pay £140 towards its reconstruction). An Act of Parliament to improve the river Welland (1570) may also have been the fruit of Cecil patronage.

But there were also disagreements both within the town and between the town and Cecil. In the 1550s, a group of burgesses wrote repeatedly to Cecil that the commissioners appointed to 'spoil' the churches made redundant by the amalgamations (especially St Stephen's united to St Michael's) acting more upon

'a peculier desier of advantage to theym selfs then eny parte tendinge to a comon welth whiche we all wyshe and desier to the pore commonwelth of Stampforde',

had disposed of their profits without consulting the Alderman or rendering account, to the grave detriment of the town. Cecil on the other hand wrote sharply to the town complaining that the borough council had burdened St Martin's parish with part of the cost of post horses, and that the borough was interfering with his grain mills, to which the Alderman made sycophantic reply, constantly beseeching Lord Burghley to show to the town 'good lordship'. There were complaints to Cecil about his tenants whom he supported, and counter-complaints about an irregular election to the office of Alderman. The Earl of Exeter became a kind of court of appeal; he nominated the town's Members of Parliament, its officials and its schoolmaster.

Having Lord Secretary Burghley living in the immediate neighbourhood, however, brought some gain with it. There were Royal visits — even in the town itself; Queen Elizabeth, debarred on one occasion (1566) from staying at Burghley House, because Cecil's daughter Ann went down with smallpox, resided at the Greyfriars in Stamford. Another house was built by the son of the Lord Treasurer at Wothorpe, just to the south of Stamford. And thus the tradition of great noble establishments in and around Stamford, seen from at least Henry VII's reign when the King's mother, Margaret of Beaufort, settled in Collyweston, six miles to the south-west, was reinforced, until in the end the town was surrounded by aristocratic seats. Some lived in Stamford, like Katherine, Duchess of Suffolk, and later the Custs at Blackfriars; others, like the Berties at Uffington and the Noels at Exton lived outside. It is thus not surprising that the town drew its elected Members of Parliament, from these families with all their connections and influence at court — five of the Cecil family held this honour between 1504 and 1589, together with relations such as Francis Harrington of Bourne and Robert Wingfield. Members of other prominent local families such as the Husseys, the Irbys, the Heneages and the Digbys of Luffenham were chosen; so too were local merchants, lawyers and others, many of them in the service of the Cecil family, such as Henry Lacy, deputy steward of the manor and Thomas Balguy, deputy for Cecil as Recorder of the borough.

The town council found themselves forced to accept the new relationship into which they now entered. What had been to a large extent a freehold town, with several prominent but loosely held ecclesiastical estates in it, under a light Royal or noble overlordship, now found itself becoming more and more (especially from the eighteenth century) a leasehold town under one landlord. There was still a good deal of freehold property; what was new was the concentration of property rights into one hand. But faced with declining trade, heavier demands from government (the wars of Elizabeth, for instance, involved the borough in taking musters and keeping the trained bands in weapons) and increasing poverty in the late sixteenth century, the borough councillors needed all the patronage they could get. And so they appealed to Lord Burghley, William Cecil, the most prominent and influential government official, of whom a contemporary wrote that he 'lived long enough to nature, and long enough to glory, but not long enough to his country'.

He did what he could for the town, but the problems went too deep. The trouble lay with the economy of the town, and indeed of the country. On the heathlands to the north of the town there was a change from wool production to corn, and clearance of the woodlands and enclosure began; barley for malt and oats for fodder came to predominate, and stock-rearing for leather and for meat increased. Already the changes had begun which were to make the fens of south Lincolnshire a centre of grazing for 'prodigious numbers of large sheep and also oxen of the largest size, the overplus and best of which goes all to the London market'.

These changes did not help Stamford which, in 1541, was listed by parliament (in an Act intended to relieve distress) as one of the 'decay'd' towns of the realm. The only healthy industries in the borough were small, highly skilled crafts employing small numbers of men and distributing their goods over a wide area, like the glass painting industry of the late fifteenth century and the bell founding industry of the Norris family in the early seventeenth century. Here was no solid basis for recovery. There were then major changes in the wool and cloth exporting trades which took the centre of the economy away from the East Coast, and this hit the town hard. But these changes do not seem to have been recognised by the town council. It still pinned its hopes on trade and on the textile industry, turning its back on the tanning of leather which might have saved Stamford and even made it into a Kettering or a Northampton. The mills, both those on the river and the windmills which lined the ridge to the north of the town, frequently fell into decay and needed extensive restoration.

The main attention then still focussed on textiles. In 1561, hemp mills were established and in 1567 foreign weavers were brought in. Lady Cecil set up a spinning school and a silk industry, neither of which lasted long. In 1582, a prominent citizen, Richard Shute gave more than £150 towards the setting up in the town of 'the profittable science and occupation of clotheinge'. Experiments in the New Draperies and canvas-making were made without great success, although flax was grown extensively in the neighbourhood. Foreigners (Walloons) were invited over, to settle and bring their crafts with them: 'these paye nothinge for their fines . . . because theire coming is for the benefit of the towne in helpinge to teache the inhabitants theire trade of weaving and spinyng'. In 1570, after the flood which swept away the bridge, the town secured an Act of Parliament to renew the Welland as a navigable river, for their eyes were still set firmly on the eastern ports rather than London, and they attributed the decline of trade to the silting up of this waterway. The Act was renewed in 1620, and throughout the seventeenth century the corporation regularly entered into new agreements with undertakers, leasing the tolls of the Navigation between Stamford, Spalding and Boston in a vain attempt to improve the waterway, so that vessels over 15 tons could make the three-day journey from Boston to the wharves in Stamford.

But here their efforts stuck. As late as 1640, despite many negotiations and false starts, the river was still not easily navigable. Stamford became a town of false starts, a talk-much-and-do-little place. In 1614 it was recorded that the whole town was gathered together

'that they might be persuaded to adventure some money according to the [Privy] Councelles letters into Virginia, but beinge not thought fitt by the greater parte of the Company there assembled to adventure to anyman's private purse nothinge was done'.

The poverty of the town was one if its notable features and prompted charitable endowments. In the 1570s the council established a poor house. Later in the century Lord Burghley re-founded the hospital of St John and St Thomas the martyr by the bridge (later known as Lord Burghley's Hospital). In 1609 his son Thomas granted the manorial rights in East and West Deeping to the corporation of the town to assist in apprenticing the youth of Stamford into various occupations, and other charities followed, at least fourteen in the years between 1585 and 1655.

But if skilled aliens were to be welcomed to Stamford, other 'furryners' (ie non-Stamfordians) were not: only local residents, not strangers, for instance, were to be employed by the inhabitants of the town; those outsiders who bought corn direct from the mills were to be stopped, and (in 1586) searchers were appointed to make diligent inquiry for newcomers, 'as this town is greatly burdened thereby, they being poor people that come', a theme heard repeatedly at this time (1564, 1568, 1586, 1591, 1600, 1619 and so on). In 1602, the town addressed a petition to the Crown to be excused their taxes. It is clear from the records that this is not just the special pleading common to many English towns at this time; poverty in Stamford was real and pressing.

Perhaps it is a sign of the insecurity of the times that so much internal disorder broke out in the later sixteenth century. Cecil's affinity was at the heart of the disturbances. In 1557, when the town council complained about the actions of one of Cecil's henchmen and tenants, one Emlyn, in annexing 'a little spong of grass' (later known as Emblyn's Close), they received a tart reply from Lord Burghley; such quarrels in a small provincial town were after all small beer. Richard Shute, a lawyer and forceful Alderman on occasion, caused trouble when he said that 'it was a great disgrace for him to be of the companie of the first twelve, as they were men of base condition . . . dolts and fooles'. Dispute over the aldermanry elections in 1590 and 1591 caused Secretary Cecil (in his capacity as Recorder of the borough) to write sharply to the town council in Pauline language: 'being compassed with one wall, differ not among yourselves . . .', followed by a long sermon on the value of concord and mutual love. The last years of the century saw street violence, law suits and a march to London for assistance in the war of factions that broke out; and in 1592 a government enquiry reported on 'such disorders as within these four years, tending almost to the utter overthrow of the said Corporation, hath been committed'. They were told that the borough records had been falsified and fighting had begun — largely, it was alleged because Cecil had ceased to be Recorder. There was trouble again on the same issue in 1597.

Not all was gloom and riots; there were still some glories. William Camden, lamenting that the town 'could never perfectly recover and come up to its former glory,' added significantly 'tho' 'tis pretty well at this time' (1586). Robert Mylles, who graced the grammar school as headmaster, was a poet of minor renown in an age of poets. Toby Norris's bells, made for more than a century (1603-1708), furnished the steeples of All Saints and St Mary's in Stamford and many churches in the neighbouring countryside. The town was the venue for the local gentry for races at least as early as 1619 and probably earlier. In 1602, when the new King James I passed through the town on his way from Scotland to St James's Palace, the town laid on a pageant and secured a new charter, with a successful plea to be excused from some of the heavy burden of taxation which still fell on it from the past: and with reason — for the costs of frequent royal visits (two occurred in successive years, 1633 and 1634) were heavy, and in 1635, at the threat of another costly visit, the Alderman and town council protested and threatened to refuse to pay the fees which the courtiers around the King and Queen demanded on each of these occasions.

These costs fell now on fewer people, for in 1604, disaster struck the town. Early in February 1604, the vicar of St George's church noted that one of the persons he buried had died of the plague, at that time raging in London. At first there was a lull, and then the full force of the outbreak was felt. Plague had been recorded in the town in earlier years, for instance in 1574 and 1581-2, but not on this scale. Throughout the summer months men, women and children died like flies. The town council did what they could to contain the outbreak. They ordered 'that a Cabbin should be erected and built wherein persons infected with the sickenes called the Plague shoulde be kepte and mayneteyned' and a special levy was taken on the town for the charges of those infected victims now housed outside the east gate. All visitors to the town were banned; those who caught the disease were ordered to stay indoors, and the healthy were told in no uncertain terms not to visit nearby infected towns; nor were residents to 'leave the town because some houses are affected with plague, on payment of fines'.

The real toll on the town is not clear. Some 600 people were registered as having been buried in 1604 instead of the more normal annual total of about 30-40 — and this must represent between a quarter and a third of the town's then population. Others moved away. By September the plague passed on and the town stood still, weakened and uncertain of the future. A good start to the new century and to the new reign!

The immediate reaction was an outburst of activity on the part of the residents to improve town amenities. A programme of more river improvements was launched and the water system (renewed in 1570) was again renewed. The council attempted to regulate building in the town more closely, and byelaws were passed with increasing frequency; concern had been expressed on several earlier occasions (1551, 1562, 1574, etc) and was now repeated about the number of persons knocking entrances through the town walls at the bottom of their gardens (especially inns), and building against the walls was discouraged in 1630. Several more charities were established at this time such as Snowden's hospital and Well's school, both of them the direct result of the plague. In 1604 the Reverend Richard Snowden established a house for seven poor widows; and in the same year when Edward Wells, a shoemaker who lived in St Peter's Street, and his wife and two children all died of the plague, he left his property to the parish to set up a petty school . . . 'for such children as should be poor and freeborn within the said town, for their virtuous education and bringing up in the fear of God, a good literature and means'. Lady Dorothy Cecil in the same year (1604) founded a further school in St Martin's.

But fear of the plague persisted and engaged the attention of the town council on several occasions in the course of the seventeenth century. One of the answers the town had to recurrent plague was to isolate itself. In 1637, when 'the infectious sickness called the plague is at this time diversely dispersed in many parts of this kingdom and some nigh us which doth put this Town both in fear and danger', diligent watch for strangers was to be kept night and day; the Alderman and council were charged with supervising this watch throughout the twenty-four hours. In 1630, four sufficient warders were to be hired 'now in the time of infection'. On the whole, the policy was successful. In July 1642, it is true, 'some houses in the Town be now infected', and several people fled the town 'because of the Plague', which caused the council concern for two reasons — that those who remained had to sustain greater burdens and, more important, 'the sight of doors and shop windows shut up' and the market 'demeaned, disgraced and forsaken' would lead visitors to imagine that the plague was rampant — so that the refugees were ordered to pay double rates for the relief of sickness in the town. But on the whole, studies of the parish registers show that the town escaped relatively unscathed. There are the occasional deaths recorded as 'of the plague', but no general outbreak. In 1655, when first London and then the neighbouring towns of Peterborough, Oundle, Crowland and Kettering were severely affected, the policy of isolation won the day. No letters, coaches, horses or travellers from London and later from these nearer towns were to be allowed into the town without a certificate from a JP that the town they came from was free from plague; no one was to attend markets in these places; and the watch was to be rigidly enforced — which steps 'by God's blessing have proved successful and our Town hitherto hath been preserved'.

Stamford therefore escaped the worst ravages of the plague in the later seventeenth century and the town began to grow again. There was an immediate up-turn in population after 1604 in every parish and, despite some set-backs, growth was maintained throughout the century. Recovery was slow but sure, although as late as 1624 the town was still described as 'poor and decayed'.

This recovery expressed itself in new buildings; timber-framed houses, neglected for even a few years as a result of death or evacuation, quickly fell into disrepair. The town council was most concerned to regulate the new building which began about this time: thus it ordered that all new habitations should be rated at no less than £1; that barns and outhouses should not be converted into tenements, nor should ancient tenements be sub-divided for habitations; and that all those who had built houses on the town wall or the ramp along the ditch outside the walls should take out leases from the town for their new property. It was not so much concern about fire, amenities or defence that gave birth to these regulations as money; all such property was to 'be fit for the dwelling of such person as shall be assessed in the subsidy at 20s in land or £3 in goods'.

The result was the emergence of the distinctive style known as 'Stamford Vernacular' — town houses, built of stone and roofed with Collyweston slate. The fronts of these houses were marked by bays — one on each side of the street door in the larger examples, and a single one in the smaller buildings. The bays ran up through both floors, sometimes finishing beneath the eaves but more usually running up into their own gable ends. Striking examples of this type of house can be seen in all parts of Stamford. A fire in the town in 1637 no doubt encouraged the use of stone rather than timber as a building material. Older houses were often given new fronts, as along the north side of St Paul's Street, but many were built from new. The rooms inside were small and low, still with exposed ceiling beams; but these houses, characteristic in many ways of the smaller towns of the limestone belt (such as Burford in Oxfordshire), were a clear improvement on the buildings which preceded them.

It was probably in the process of this rebuilding that Stamford's antiquarianism developed into a major theme in the town's consciousness. Speed's map of the town (c1600) was openly archaic, searching for lost mediaeval sites; probably it sprang from or led to one of the earliest historical descriptions of Stamford, written by Brian Twyne of Oxford in the first years of the seventeenth century after a visit to the town; while in 1646 Richard Butcher, innkeeper and former town clerk, wrote his *Survey of Stamford,* an early example of urban local history.

Housing was not the only matter which concerned the town council. Trade was at the core of the borough's economy; industry was less highly regarded. Legislation against the nuisances of 'ovens' probably refers to the iron-smelting kilns and tannery vats which were present within the town walls as well as to bakehouses. Leather was ordered to be sold at the Guildhall in the Monday market, and new stalls were provided outside the church in the centre of High Street, St Michael the Greater. A new attempt to establish a spinning school was made in 1634, and the mills, especially Hudd's Mill (which belonged to the corporation) and King's Mill (the Earl of Exeter's prerogative mill) were rebuilt.

These mills were one (but not the only) source of the constant disputes between the town and the town's overlords. The Cecils insisted against fierce opposition that most of the inhabitants of the town should grind their corn and malt in their mills or pay for the privilege of a more speedy service elsewhere. But other issues also caused friction. There was bitter controversy over the borough charters, which were renewed in 1638 and again in 1641; over who had the right to lease the corporation mills (an important part of the town economy at that time); over brewing rights (the numerous maltsters ganged together against new and restrictive orders imposed by the Earl of Stamford in asserting his monopoly in the 1630s). Time and again the Recorder or his deputy, and the steward or his deputy were challenged by the council or by groups of citizens in the execution of their duties — or so they alleged whenever they appealed to the Privy Council for assistance and remedy. But without success; the Privy Council supported the Earl of Stamford and the Cecils. The Earl cut a new mill channel across the town meadows; he took a toll on the market stalls; and if challenged, he 'toss'd the best burgesses out of their gownes'. Richard Butcher should have known, for he had suffered from the man he came to regard as 'the towne's common enemy'.

There were religious rumblings too. Lord Exeter's influence in the town did not prevent the emergence of a nascent form of puritanism, led by John Vicars at St Mary's church. His antics and opinions led to a public trial and humiliation in 1631: he berated the town councillors for condoning the breaking of the Sabbath and his own parishioners for their worldly way of life, and he established at St Mary's church an alternative congregation drawn as much from outside the town as from within. Before his condemnation, his Calvinist views on all matters (even the King's foreign policy) split the town and forced first the Bishop and then the Court of High Commission to intervene. Others were tainted with puritanism; Thomas Hatcher of Careby, one of the town's MPs from 1628 was an amateur theologian, later to serve in the Civil Wars as Colonel Hatcher and governor of Lincoln for the parliamentary forces.

The town's members of parliament played a significant part in the struggles which were to follow. They reveal the divided allegiances within the borough. The Earl of Stamford, for instance, was a parliamentarian even though the town was on the whole loyalist. John Weaver of North Luffenham, a freeman of the borough, became a soldier in the Earl of Manchester's army, MP for Stamford in 1645 and 'one of the most outspoken members of the independent party' in the Long Parliament. He was appointed to the commission to try Charles I, although he never served in this capacity. MP for the town for all parliaments up to 1659, he held the Tower of London against the returning Charles II in 1660. On the other hand, Geoffrey Palmer of Carlton, Northants, lawyer and MP for Stamford in 1640, who took part in the impeachment of Strafford, joined the King's party and was imprisoned after being involved in a disturbance in the House of Commons. He attended the Royalist parliament of 1643-4; in 1655 he was again imprisoned in the Tower for threatening to raise troops against the government of the day. On the Restoration of Charles II, he was knighted and appointed Attorney-general. In these two persons may be seen the polarity which faced the more humble inhabitants of Stamford.

Despite the careers of Hatcher, Weaver and the Earl of Stamford, Puritanism was not really endemic in the town. On the whole it was Royalist in sympathy, neither Laudian nor dissenting in ecclesiastical practice, nor so loyal that a visit from the King in 1632 (when the town council gave him a present of a silver and gilded cup to express their devotion and ordered all houses on both sides of the street through which the King would pass to be white-washed) did not result in some complaining, and in a sharp letter from Lord Exeter to the town, exhorting the inhabitants to entertain the King fittingly. Charles I was on occasion tactless in the way he treated his supporters. Stamford suffered the taxation, the musters and the billetting of soldiers and officials, grudgingly, as befitted a town with a Royal past; but when the crunch came, it declared for the King. The trained band was called out and some of the burgesses fought for the King in the wars of the 1640s which swept over and through Stamford on several occasions. 'The King's Arms' wrote Stukeley 'were done upon the gable end of a house in [St Martins] in which Charles I lodged soon after the battle of Naseby', and another house in Barn Hill formerly belonging to the Wolph family provided the King with shelter and a route of escape from his enemies. Early in 1643, the town (along with Grantham and Peterborough) was captured for parliament: as it was reported on 27 July 1643

'Col. Cromwell . . . hath taken Stamford and Burleigh House, a great receptacle for the Newark Cavaliers for their in-road into Northamptonshire and parts thereabouts: the service, it is informed, was somewhat difficult — but it was taken with the loss of very few men, and many prisoners of note taken, amongst the rest, two colonels, six or seven captains, 400 foot, and about 200 horse, great store of arms, and abundance of rich pillage'

but the garrison from Belvoir Castle relieved it despite the defence conducted by Thomas Lord Grey, the son of the town's lord, the Earl of Stamford, both of whom were on the side of parliament in those troubled years. In July Burghley House was seized by Cromwell and the town of Stamford 'cleared' of Royalists; in the next year, parliament's forces under the Earl of Manchester garrisoned the town, but by June it was once again Royalist; in August 1645 the parliamentary forces were back again. It was alleged that there was some damage caused in all of this — that Cromwell for instance destroyed the Eleanor Cross which stood in Scotgate during one of his visits in 1643 and 1644, though Butcher, writing in 1645, suggests that it was still standing then.

The life of the town was disrupted in other ways in the 1640s. Already the bitter fight against the Royal grant to the Earl of Stamford of a monopoly of brewing ale had led to resignations and dismissals among the town's councillors and officers. Now the borough council was purged. In 1645 the Earl of Manchester ejected all the town's parish clergy and introduced 'preaching ministers' in their place, while in the previous year the rector of St John's church was charged with popery, on the grounds that the glass in his church windows still contained objectionable images. The benefices were sequestered and St Mary's parish library was plundered. A rising led by a number of Royalists in or near the town (Richard Wolph, the resident who had sheltered the King on an earlier occasion, Dr Michael Hudson, the indefatigable King's servant and rector of Uffington, and the Reverend Thomas Stiles of Crowland), together with John Ashurnham of Sussex, leading to the capture of Woodcroft House near Eton, resulted in a further extensive series of dismissals by the Committee of Indemnity from the borough council in 1648.

Stamford's fortunes under the Commonwealth and Protectorate are not clear. Troops were on occasion mustered in the town, but in the absence of a king, its loyalty was not in doubt. Royalist estates were surveyed, sequestered and just as quickly redeemed. Some attempts were made to impose puritan standards on the town. The races were abolished (as elsewhere in the country); a limited number of licences was issued to victualling houses in the town. From 1653 a single lay 'register', Richard Royce, served as parish clerk to all the six parishes to record all the births, deaths and civil marriages in the town.

Plans were drawn up for the amalgamation of some of these parishes into a smaller number, largely on the grounds of poverty and the small size of some of the parishes, but it was never carried out. Certainly St Mary's benefice was so poor that, during the early years of the century, there was great difficulty in filling it, at least one incumbent having left it and 'gone into Ireland and has there taken a new benefice' (1638). This activity did not however stop the discontent in the town, and a demonstration refusal to pay the poor and church rates led to further government intervention (1655).

Nor did the presence of preaching ministers prevent the population from claiming in 1659 that a miracle — a healing by an angelic visitant — had happened within the borough, a claim supported by at least one of the new breed of ministers in the town's pulpits. And the new and purged borough council maintained something of its own independent line; it even expressed its civic consciousness in a new Guildhall in the Monday Market (St Mary's Place) in 1655. Nevertheless the impression which the records give at this time is one of waiting for the inevitable — the collapse of the Interregnum and the Restoration of the King which took place in 1660.

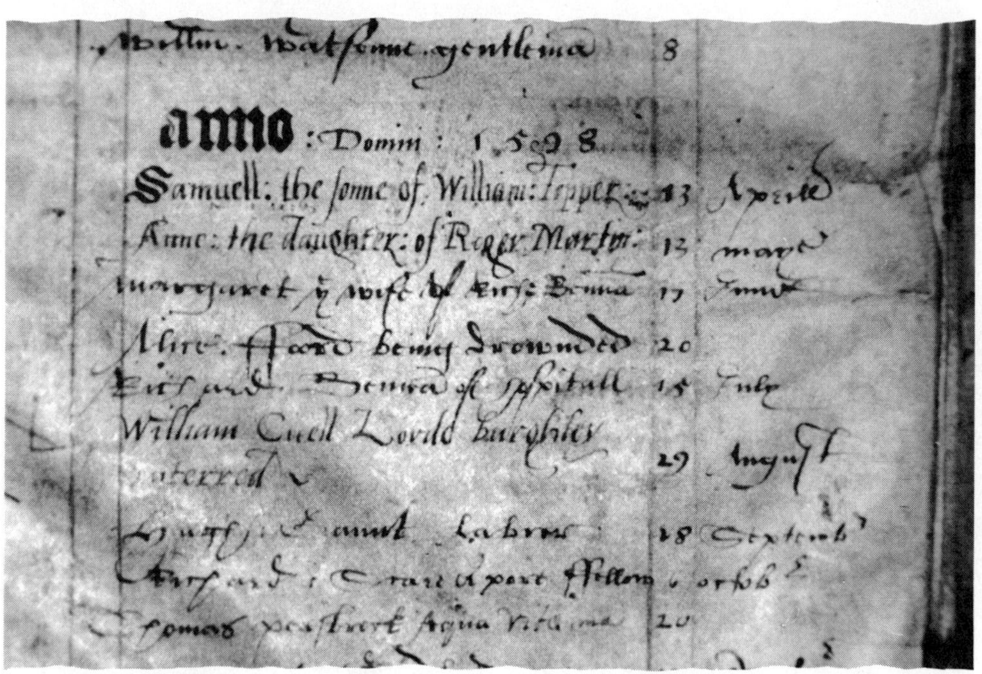

Extract from St Martin's parish register recording the burial of William Cecil, Lord Burghley, 1598.

ABOVE: Burghley House, finished 1588, engraving by Jenkinson, 1891;
BELOW: the Burghley tombs in St Martin's church; LEFT: Richard
Cecil and Jayne his wife 1552; RIGHT: William Cecil, Lord Burghley.

LEFT: Tomb of Sir David Phillips in St Mary's church. RIGHT: Hospital founded by Lord Burghley c1597. BELOW: Speed's map of Stamford, c1600.

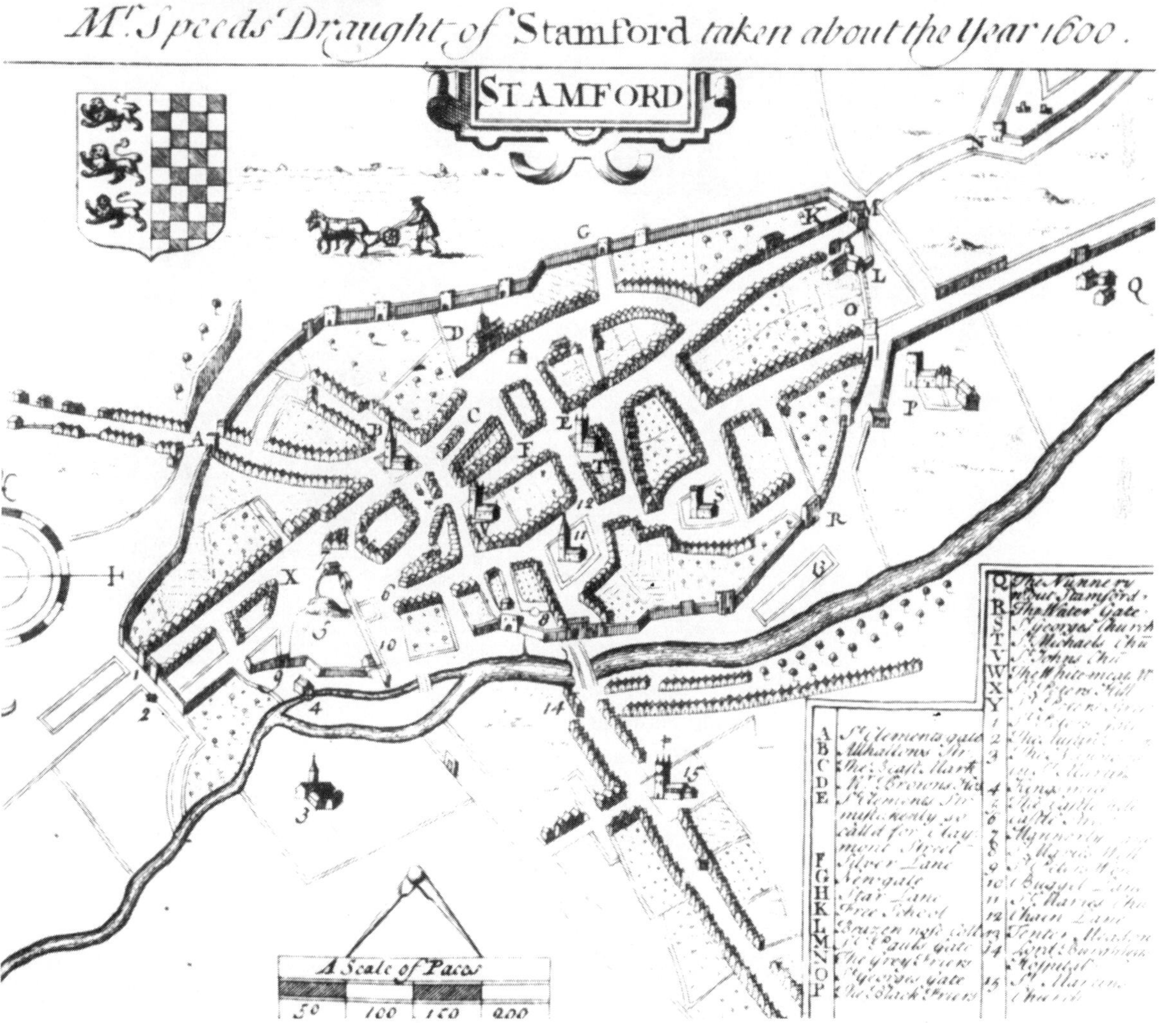

Guildhall built over the bridge.

Half-timbered housing: LEFT: St Mary's Street (east); RIGHT: St Mary's Street (west); BELOW: vernacular housing of sixteenth and seventeenth centuries: in Gas Lane (now destroyed). (BL)

Vernacular housing of sixteenth and seventeenth centuries: LEFT: High Street (now destroyed); BELOW; High Street St Martin's; ABOVE: St Paul's Street (north side); CENTRE: St Paul's Street (south side).

ABOVE: Tudor Inn, The Bull and Swan in St Martin's; LEFT: a town of narrow lanes: near St Mary's church; (BL) RIGHT: extracts from parish register: burials in St George's parish.

Parish registers: LEFT: plague burials, St George's parish, 1604; RIGHT: plague burials, St Michael's parish, 1604; BELOW: fully developed Stamford vernacular house, St Martin's. (BL)

Grandeur 1660-1800

God send the kingdome better for to fare
And then, I hope, Stamford will have a share
In that well-being. Let us all repent,
Then God, no doubt, in mercy will relent,
And make our cities and our townes to shine
Againe in glory, earthly and divine.
Heav'n grant the same: and, till the dooming day,
May they and Stamford rest in joy alway.

Richard Butcher, 1646

Early in the reign of the restored Charles II, Daniel Wigmore, a wealthy merchant, county justice of the peace, mercer and woollen draper, and canal builder, three times mayor of Stamford, asked the builder of the newly finished Lyndon Hall in Rutland (perhaps John Sutton of Stamford) to design a new house for him in St George's Square. The house (now No 19) was completed in 1674 and its appearance marks a turning point in Stamford's fortunes. Towering at that time above its more humble neighbours with four floors of rooms over a basement, it could afford the luxury of a hipped roof and tall chimneys. Faced with finely dressed stone (although the rear was built more coarsely) and with ornamental door, it represented all that was new and grand in contemporary building. The house still incorporated some traditional features; the front door for instance opened into a living room rather than into an entrance hall, and the large window openings were made up of small mullioned and transomed openings. But in its panelled rooms and high ceilings, decorated cross-beams and ornamental fireplaces, Wigmore's house contrasted sharply with the smaller traditional houses still being erected in the town.

The building of this house marked a new era in Stamford's history more surely than the improvements beginning in other facets of the town's appearance, such as the inspection and repair in 1667 of the town walls after the damage and neglect caused by the disturbances of the previous thirty years, or the provision of a new water supply in 1666. As with London and elsewhere, there may have been behind much of this new building activity, some fear of fire, for parts of Stamford had been burned down in 1635, and in 1675, the year after the erection of Wigmore's new house, another fire apparently hit the town, for the council issued new building regulations aimed at preventing fires. But much more likely it was a simple question of prestige. Wigmore's wealth and position called for a measure of ostentation which he proudly provided for himself and his town.

Whatever the cause, the new style caught on. It is true that some smaller houses continued to be built in something like the traditional style, although apparently the 'bay', characteristic of the Stamford Vernacular style, became less frequent; a house in St Leonard's Street, dated 1685, shows this modified tradition, contrasting sharply with the Vernacular house next door, rebuilt in 1662.

But elsewhere throughout the town, large new houses were erected, each of them more 'up-to-date' than the last, and older buildings were given a new Georgian-style facade. The face of Stamford was changed, so that today the town presents the image of an eighteenth century social centre rather than of the mediaeval town which at heart it still is. Celia Fiennes saw this process during an early stage of its development: 'Stamford town is as fine a built town all of stone as may be seen . . . much finer than Cambridge'. And social centre the town became. Gentry from all around now moved into the town, both for its amenities and for the profits which residence could offer. Thus, for example, Francis Wingfield the lawyer, prominent at the court of Charles II, had a house in St Martin's, and Sir Christopher Clapham lived in Barn Hill; the Cust family still possessed Blackfriars (to the south-east of the town), while around the town the Finchs of Burley on the Hill and the Heathcotes of Stretton joined the Noel family and other landed families building up large estates and looking to Stamford for goods, amenities and social contact.

The struggles that emerged over the parliamentary elections of the 1670s reveal some of the newer gentry influences on the town. In 1676 the Noels of Exton (later Lords Gainsborough) fielded one candidate, the Hatchers of Careby the other. The Earls of Exeter (Cecils) and of Stamford (Greys), Baptist Noel, Lord Campden (father of the later Earl of Gainsborough) and John Egerton, Earl of Bridgewater distributed their favours between the two candidates. Robert Bertie, Earl of Lindsey and Lord-lieutenant of Lincolnshire, with his relations Lord Willoughby and Charles Bertie, played a decisive part in securing the election of Henry Noel, including in the process the holding of a muster of the Kesteven militia in the town; and when in the following year (1677) Henry Noel died suddenly, Charles Bertie of Uffington, the Earl's brother, was secured as one of the town's MPs without an election. Behind this struggle lay 'a high contest of that country, [Lincolnshire] between Lord Lindsey and Sir Robert Carr'. In 1679, Carr's party briefly defeated Lindsey in Stamford, but Sir Robert Carr died in 1683 and, two years later, Lindsey secured the election of his two brothers Charles and Peregrine Bertie as MPs for the town, in the first parliament of the new and Catholic King James II (1685).

The Bertie influence on the town was thus strong. In the purge of borough privileges conducted by Charles II, Stamford secured new charters (1685) with the support of the Lindsey family, and Peregrine and Charles Bertie were nominated to the town council, while Robert, Earl of Lindsey was named in the charters as Recorder of the borough. New regalia were presented to the corporation so that 'the citizens of Stamford may celebrate . . . their friendship to the house of Bertie'. In this, they were supported by Lord Campden and opposed by the Cecils and Greys. Disputes over elections and borough offices persisted until 1688 when the Cecils and the Berties agreed to nominate one MP each, and between them to control the borough council. There were Whigs, of course: the Cust family who lived at Blackfriars, just outside the town hall to the east, opposed these candidates in 1679, 1688 and 1695 and virtually bankrupted themselves in the process, being successful only in the first of these elections and then only with the support of the Cecil family. The town was split by the bloodless Revolution of 1688 which deposed James II, the general populace (like the Berties) declaring for William III, but the mayor attempting to dampen their celebrations; and throughout the last decade of the seventeenth century, the Jacobite Cecils found some supporters in Stamford, although for the moment the loyalist Berties reigned supreme in the town.

The borough council was overawed in the face of these great men. The office of Recorder was traditionally reserved for one or other of the nobility, who served it by deputy. Thus the Royalist Lord Campden of Exton held it from 1676 until his death in 1682 and Lord Exeter thereafter. On the Restoration of Charles II the First and Second Twelve, the two chambers of the town council, were 'purged'; in 1662, commissioners appointed for Stamford under the 'Act for the well regulatinge and governinge of corporacions'(who included Richard Noel and Francis Wingfield) dismissed two comburgesses and no less than eleven capital burgesses for 'refusinge the several oathes, declarasion and subscription tendered unto them'; and several officials, including Richard Royce, who held the posts of register, public ale-taster and sergeant at mace, together with the Master of the House of Correction, were dismissed and replaced with others of more loyalist sympathies. But despite this and several later episodes when the membership of the corporation was amended to secure greater political control, the real power in the town lay with the various noble interests and especially with their stewards, men like George Hill of St John's parish who was appointed in 1660 steward of the restored Earl of Stamford and served as Alderman (or mayor, as the chief officer was called from 1663) in the following year, or Thomas Hurst of St George's parish who succeeded him, or Edward Curtis of All Saints parish, steward of the Noel Earls of Gainsborough, who engaged prominently in land dealings and local controversies within the town; all three were lawyers.

The council was left to deal with matters relating to the social and economic development of the town. They could of course draw upon the nobility for subscriptions, but in general they were left to their own devices within limited areas of less politically important activities. They faced plague in 1665 in the neighbourhood and closed the town, setting a watch at every gate during the fairs and insisting on the production of a certificate from a local JP to say that the visitor came from an area as yet uninfected; while 'the postmaster . . . shall not permitt or suffer any persons coming from London to stay or remain in his house'. The self-imposed restrictions seem to have been successful, for the population of the town, which stood in 1676 at about 1600, rose more or less without interruption until the middle of the following century to about 2,500 despite a severe outbreak of smallpox in the summer of 1716 and further outbreaks in 1766 and 1769, in marked contrast to similar sized neighbouring towns like Bourne.

Regulation of the fairs absorbed a good deal of the town council's attention. An additional fair was granted by the King in a new charter of 1685, at the instance of Robert Bertie, Earl of Lindsey, and in 1714 two new fairs were secured from Queen Anne, again with Bertie patronage. The result was an annual cycle of great events which boosted the permanent population of the town many times over. A horse fair early in February prepared the way for the main Mid-Lent or Town Fair which lasted for two weeks; early in May came the next, followed by another later that same month or early in June (depending when Trinity Sunday fell). A fifth occured in early August and a sixth in November. Four major cattle markets (in January, September, October and December) had many features characteristic of the fairs. Colour, noise and (no doubt) other less pleasing sensations were added to the life of the inhabitants of Stamford by this round of activity. Scattered through the streets of Stamford, these trading occasions formed the focal points of the town's calendar and a source of prosperity and perennial disorder. As one jaundiced observer wrote of them about 1667:

> 'To Stamford came I, where I find
> Purses are sold of every kind;
> Purses there are that cut a flash,
> Purses in plenty, but no cash;
> As many vermin as crawl o'er mee
> So many beggars are before ye.
> Where are the scholars, proctor, fellows, college?
> They've into purses cramm'd their former knowledge.'

A shortage of currency provided the town under Daniel Wigmore, its mayor, with an opportunity to raise funds. In 1667, the town agreed that it would put in hand 'the coyninge of halfe pence to goe in the towne, and that this benefit which shall be made by them shall redownd to the poore, and that they shall be changed by the overseers'. Two years later, the 'benefit' was to be 'leyd out for and towards the repairing of the Guildhall' which the council leased from the Earl of Exeter.

In 1668 the council had rebuilt Brazenose House, apparently intending to use it for their own functions, but in the end it was first leased and then used for charitable purposes.

In 1682, the mayor and corporation were accused of not suppressing conventicles as they ought: the council agreed that any action brought against the mayor 'for denying to assist him [William Hawkins, an informer] in suppressing conventicles . . . shall be discharged and defrayed att the public charge of the corporacion . . . '. Nonconformity was not strong in Stamford, but it was resented; in 1704, a total of 17 nonconformists were recorded in the town out of a population of about 2,000-2,500. The presence of a Presbyterian conventicle in St Paul's Street aroused hostility, for memories of John Vicars at St Mary's church were not yet dead. In any case, a 'high church' reaction was apparent in the town at this time: in 1693, for instance, a petition was presented to the Bishop for the removal of the communion table in St Michael's church 'from the body of the chancel to the east end'. Dissenters were clearly regarded as both politically and religiously undesirable, especially when such a conventicle drew its congregation of between a hundred and a hundred and fifty from many miles around. The chapel was thus burned down in a riot in 1714; but a new chapel in Star Lane was opened some six years later. The records are silent on the presence of organised groups of Quakers, Baptists or Papists in the town at the start of the eighteenth century.

Meanwhile the town, on the basis of its role as a trading centre for the region and with noble support, was equipping itself with the houses, shops, public buildings and amenities of a major social centre. The inns were already famous: Daniel Defoe on his visit in 1724 'stopp'd at the George out of curiosity, because it is reckoned one of the greatest Inns in England'. The town's water supply demanded constant attention and was renewed in 1690 and again in 1697 (when an engineer from St Albans was commissioned to bring water from the river to the town centre and thence by pipes to individual houses as requested), while in 1722 a bath house was built between the castle and the river for common use. An Assembly Room was built about 1717, to house the increasingly popular assemblies held in Barn Hill, and the town's papers are full of advertisements of the services of dancing masters. Plays were performed in the town throughout the eighteenth century, first at the Guildhall (as early as 1698 and on into the new century) and later in the Theatre built between 1766 and 1768, 'after the manner of the London Theatres . . . [and] reckoned the completest place of its size in the kingdom', and linked into the Midland circuit based on Leicester rather than into the Lincoln circuit. Both of these, like the Subscription Library, were provided by private entrepreneurs for profit. Lord Exeter built the cockpit in the George Hotel in St Martin's, south of the river, to complement the fights which took place in the White Swan, the Red Lion Pit, the Half Moon, the Roebuck ('between the gentlemen of Lincolnshire and the gentlemen of Northamptonshire', 1738) and elsewhere in the town. Other amenities benefitting a self-respecting town of the period flourished — billard tables (despite council ordinances against them from as early as 1665), a bowling green outside the west gate as early as 1712, and coffee rooms. Card assemblies and balls were held, cricket was played, concerts attended and the may-pole in St Mary's parish decorated. Outdoors there was fox-hunting, now organised into meets and hounds. One major event climaxed the year for the gentles, the June races (originally Mid-Lent) held in various venues but eventually settling down on Wittering Heath to the south of the town, where a new Grandstand was erected in 1766. Race week was accompanied by plays, concerts, assemblies, cockfights and other social events. Races were of course held at other times — in March and October, often to coincide with the fairs, and the army paraded and exercised on the course as well. For the commonalty, the races were matched by the ancient sport of bull-running in November and occasionally at other times. With its own newspapers, the *Stamford Post* (1710-11?) and the *Stamford Mercury* (which, dating from at least 1714, may or may not be the oldest surviving provincial newspaper in the country) published every market day (Friday), its Newsroom and Library established in 1787, with its complement of town waits, Stamford was apparently equipped with everything needful for its prosperity. As Daniel Defoe saw it in 1724, it was 'a very fair, well-built, considerable and wealthy town'.

The town then, in the middle of the eighteenth century when the Cecils recovered its lordship from the Earl of Stamford, presented all the appearance of a major social centre for the gentry of the neighbourhood. New houses were still being built in the grand style to match in a rather more refined way some of the best examples of the early years of the century. A house in All Saints Place (No 3), built about 1716, represents perhaps the best that Stamford could offer; but more came along all over the town. Some of the facades were 'rustic' in style, heavily moulded and with a feeling of coarseness about them; others were put up by local builders to hide earlier buildings now felt to be unworthy of their surroundings. Few of the complete buildings were designed by nationally known architects (George Portwood and William Legg may be exceptions); most of them came straight from the pattern books available to builders and clients at the time. And there were few attempts to build whole terraces, crescents or squares of new Georgian houses as at Bath and elsewhere; Stamford was a town of separate tenements. When the ninth Earl of Exeter came to start on his programme of systematic (if piecemeal) redevelopment (he developed no less than seven separate sites in the town) towards the end of the eighteenth century, his work was plainer and (despite its scale) humbler in character than similar building in other towns. As the rows of buildings erected on the corner of St Mary's Hill and St Mary's Street show, Stamford by the 1780s had lost the race to keep up with the best that was available elsewhere. Lord Exeter's attempt was noble and on a large scale, but it failed.

This was the town which the Cecil family took over once more in the middle of the eighteenth century. Lord Exeter's interest in Stamford so far had been largely that of a landholder; but it began to go further than that from the 1730s. An attack on the Bertie dominance in the parliamentary elections for Stamford was begun in 1727. The quarrel came to a head in the 1734 elections, when the Cecils joined once more with the Noel family of Exton to oust the Berties. The town was flooded with outsiders who were alleged to have the vote; bribes were paid and voters and officials were intimidated by both sides. Lord Exeter was supported by Francis Howgrave, who had taken charge of the *Stamford Mercury* in 1732; and in 1737-8 the rival factions came to blows over the post of warden of Browne's Hospital. Finally in 1747, Lord Exeter purchased the lordship of the manor of Stamford from the Earls of Stamford for just under £7,000 and the town settled down under new management; in eighteenth-century Stamford, it was patronage which counted.

It was however a town of strong social coherence. At the heart was a small group of lawyers, such as the Curtis family, who exercised a tight hold over the leasing and sub-leasing of houses, shops and inns throughout the town. The councillors, like Alderman Williamson, who refronted his mediaeval house in St Mary's Street in the new style, or Alderman Feast, who collected ancient carved stone for his house in St Peter's Street, lived in style. A group of quarrelling antiquarians centred on Maurice Johnson, a Spalding solicitor who successfully established the Spalding Gentlemen's Society in 1712 and tried less successfully to establish a similar 'Stamford Society'; the arrogant doctor and vicar of All Saints 1730-48 and chaplain to the Duke of Ancaster, William Stukeley ('In . . . Stamford, there was not one person, clergy or lay, that had any taste or love of learning and ingenuity') with his pretentious 'Brazenose Society', and Francis Peck who compiled a valuable account of the town's mediaeval records, and others, invited visitors to the town to admire its 'ancient charms'. Buildings were identified (often wrongly) with past events; fragments of masonry and glass were shamelessly transferred from site to site, and mythical accounts of the past created for the delectation of the newly cultured citizenry. A lot of time and ingenuity was expended on a search for the lost Eleanor Cross.

Among the 'almanacks' for Stamford, such as those published between 1690 and 1796 by the Wing family, 'calculated according to Act and referred to the horizon of the antient and renowned Borough-Town of Stamford', was one produced in 1704 by Joseph Pepper. A prolific writer on many subjects including a broadsheet on the eclipse of the sun (1724) and *A Voyage to the Moon with an account of the Religion, Laws and Customs, and Manner of Government among the Lunars or Moonmen; also a description of the Country, and the Palaces of their Princes, together with their Language, and the Ceremonies used at the Funerals of their deceas'd, by a native of Spain* (1718), Pepper was one of a growing number of schoolmasters in Stamford in the eighteenth century. They announced their services in the *Stamford Mercury* and drew their clientele from the region around. The town council still managed 'the free school' under the easy eye of the master of St John's College, Cambridge, but it was on occasion the source of some dispute and embarrassment. On one occasion the school lampooned the mayor with bad Latin verse and thus created a series of complaints which lasted for more than a year. The appointment of schoolmaster was regularly an occasion of 'electioneering' and the exercise of patronage, as in every other sphere of the town's life then, and the council lost a law-suit brought by the schoolmaster for retaining and misappropriating to its own use the school endowments. Apart from the Grammar School, there were the Wells Petty School and the Bluecoat School (started in 1704) in the corporation's building of Brazenose, as well as numerous private academies advertised regularly in the *Mercury*: a French minister taught French in his boarding school in 1716; Mrs Sympson ran a school in St Martin's in 1745 and Mrs Snow in Barn Hill, and there were many others, like Mr Godman's Classical, Commercial and Mathematical Academy, or the school run by the Rector of St George's church or the school in the Congregational Chapel at the end of the century.

Education was only one of the services provided in the town for the neighbourhood. The town's banks such as Eaton, Cayley and Co, (which issued its own notes), Bellairs and Edwards & Harper, provided credit and on occasion financial assistance to set up industry. Stamford lawyers managed the land market and acted as stewards and agents to neighbouring estates. George Denshire of Stamford, who lived in a house adjoining Browne's Hospital, served as clerk of the peace to Kesteven from 1727 to 1777. The town was closely tied into the region, so that the solicitors Edward Curtis or Maurice Johnson were as well known in Spalding or Boston as they were in Stamford, and Portwood and Legg and other Stamford builders worked on developments in the neighbouring counties. In 1746-7, when an outbreak of cattle distemper in the area aroused government concern, advertisements were put in the *Stamford Mercury* closing all seven fairs and markets in Kesteven county.

But it was from trade rather than services that the wealth of the town was drawn. Gentility and trade were not mutually exclusive in the late eighteenth century: as one advertiser put it in 1790, Stamford was 'a very genteel town, and an excellent market for fish, flesh and every other conveniency'. Apart from the 'normal' trades and crafts, Stamford was full of shops specialising in many different commodities. Apothecaries such as the Woodroffes in Red Lion Square lived next door to cabinet makers and brushmakers. Boniface Bywater, clockmaker and gunsmith in St Mary's Street, advertised in the *Mercury* in 1718 for the recovery of 'a silver watch, made by Holland, London, as appears by the dial plate', stolen by his servant. The grocery shops in the High Street were full of the more exotic wares: 'black millstones, marble gravestones, Dutch matting, French brandy as cheap as from London, Red and White wines' and so on (*Mercury*, 1731). Stamford was the place to go to buy 'all sorts of silks', 'rich damasks' and other fabrics: 'all sorts of cutlery ware, scented powder wash balls, castile soap, white and yellow buttons; coffee mills, all sorts of fine Tea, chocolate made of the best nuts and snuff' (as the 'Tea Canister' at the north end of Cheyne Lane advertised in 1728); 'a great choice of Delf, best Flint Glasses, and all sorts of Potters ware' (1741).

The importance of the trading community was recognised in 1785 by the introduction of a monthly Trade Assembly — perhaps at the same time (along with the tea and card rooms added to the Assembly Rooms in 1793-4) a sign of a decline in the support of these assemblies from the traditional 'gentle' classes. Certainly the traders came to dominate the town. They built the largest houses and occupied the office of mayor throughout the century: as the head boy of Stamford School said in a public oration, the mayor of the town in 1726 was a 'seller of bacon and cheese, rope and sacking'. From 1727 to the end of the century, at least thirty-one different traders were represented among the occupations of the holder of the office of mayor; while mercers predominated, grocers, bakers, curriers, saddlers, maltsters, hatters, plumbers, tanners and ropers served alongside silversmiths and apothecaries; 'gentlemen' served as mayor on six occasions in the hundred years after 1727, among the tradesmen, craftsmen and merchants of the town.

A study of the admissions to the freedom of the borough for the years 1663 to 1721 reveals something of the changes in the town since the sixteenth century. The records of these admissions have their limitations in describing the town's full economy — less than a third of all the admissions recorded (1094) have no occupations given. Hesitations about them when discussing the burgesses in the late mediaeval town are still valid, but other considerations may now have come into play. For instance, it seems to be true by this date that admission to the freedom of the borough had become necessary on acquiring some urban houses which were rateable — a suggestion which may help to account for the number of women who were admitted with some such designation as 'widow' or with no designation at all.

Nevertheless, even within these limitations, the figures (though smaller) are revealing. Out of 706 named occupations, the biggest group (19%) was now the victuallers. Another group to improve its relative position was the builders (12.4%). But entries with social designations (5.6%) and the service industries (11.4%) had strikingly increased. The metal workers were slightly more numerous (6.3%), but their ranks now included some luxury industries like clockmakers rather than the bell founders of the previous century (the foundry closed in the early years of the eighteenth century). Textile workers (including weavers) were still numerous (17.2%), although they were proportionally less significant than before. Leather workers (12.9%) dropped further. The small industry of arms manufacture in the late mediaeval town (fletchers, bowyers and armourers) had vanished altogether, as had almost all the agriculturalists. Labourers too declined to 13.2%.

Perhaps however the character of the town is shown most revealingly in the types of services recorded. Apart from the significant number of builders with their glaziers, plumbers and painters, the gardeners and seedsmen, there were pipemakers, perfumers, coachmen, booksellers, printers and stationers, a writingmaster, and large numbers of apothecaries. Among the victuallers were confectioners and gingerbread makers; a ribbon weaver occurred among the textile workers, milliners among the retailers, and there were watchmakers, spectaclemakers and cabinet makers. The horse races were perhaps reflected in the farriers and the horse coursers. In other words, the list reflects the nature of the town as a social centre. Perhaps it is no accident that no less than five peers were admitted to the freedom although they paid no fine for entry.

What is clear is that a potential industrial base for the town, seen earlier as either textile or leather working, had failed to produce lasting results. Only the iron-founding of the seventeenth century continued, with a new foundry established in 1771 on the fields to the north of the town. But industry on any large scale was missing. Instead, the town had become a social market centre for a large area around. Goods on sale in the High Street 'may be had (if desired) at Bourne every Saturday and at Market Deeping every Wednesday'. Carriers left the Red Lion in Butcher Row or the White Hart in Maiden Lane, carrying newspapers and goods to the villages of the neighbouring counties, and carriers from nearby towns made regular journeys to Stamford. Stamford became a collecting centre for the delivery of goods to the London markets: 'For the conveniency of Gentlemen who have occasion to send venison from Stamford, Oakham, Uppingham, Oundle and any other places adjacent, to London. There will be sent Pack-horses or Carts from the Bell Inn in the Butcher-row in Stamford every Tuesday morning . . .' (1728). Daily posts were instituted by 1762, serving not just the town but the region. Coaches with names like *The Stamford Fly* or *The Old Stamford Coach*, *The Regent* or *The Truth and Daylight*, left the various inns of Stamford for London, Cambridge, Lincoln, York and Edinburgh and all places in between. The goods produced locally, the 'prodigious numbers of large sheep and also oxen of the largest size' reared in the region around Stamford, as Defoe noted, 'goes all to the London market'.

The road, then — the Great North Road — was the blood-stream of Stamford's prosperity. The river was still important. It was leased out by the town council (and probably re-dug) in 1664, and thereafter continuously throughout the eighteenth century improvements were carried out between Stamford and Spalding. Traffic (mainly agricultural produce, stone from the quarries and malt sent out in exchange for coal and groceries) flowed along it, and men like Bartholomew Margerum of Deeping St James, waterman 'who usually carried goods from Boston to Stamford and other places', complained of the high tolls levied on goods which used the Navigation. Profits were made, however; in 1676 the Earl of Exeter built a new wharf on the St Martin's side of the river, where maltings also developed. Nevertheless the drainage works being carried out in the fens between Stamford and the coast spelled the end of a useful life for the Welland Navigation; although several shops had warehouses on the riverside, trade declined on the river.

Its place was taken by The Road for both regional and long-distance travel and transport. By 1769, the stage-coach journey to London, which in 1685 cost twenty shillings and took two days, was now only sixteen shillings ('inside') and took one day. The links with the capital meant that Stamford was the first place in the county to enjoy the new fashions; it was the first town to have a theatre, permanent race course and Assembly Rooms. The 'abundance of very good inns' in Stamford, on which Daniel Defoe commented, showed the newer north-south orientation which replaced the earlier east-west pattern (although the town still continued to look, as it had always done, more to Leicester than to Lincoln). Some of the most important of these inns and hotels have now gone — the Bull between High Street and St Mary's Street, the Bluebell off Ironmonger Street, the Old Swan (later the Swan and Talbot) in St Mary's Street, and the George and Angel, facing the rise of St Mary's Hill and looking over the bridge and the route from the south. The George Hotel was extensively rebuilt in the last few years of the century, at a cost of over £1,800. The roads were not always safe, of course; highwaymen became an increasing menace. In 1744, the postboy was robbed of the Stamford, Bourne and Peterborough mails near Stilton; and in 1755 one Rogers, a highwayman, was committed to Stamford gaol. Legends of Dick Turpin were not unknown in Stamford.

The turnpike system was in part a device to make the roads safer as well as more convenient for travel. The stretch of road to the north of Stamford, between the Welland and the town of Grantham, was improved in 1739, and the stretch to the south, to Wansford, ten years later. Further improvements to the local road system were made in the later eighteenth century; in 1756, the road to Bourne was taken over by a Stamford-based turnpike trust, and eventually no less than eight roads around the town were under the control of a group of six trusts, most of them run by the same men. A new turnpike Act was secured in 1776 which affected the streets in the town itself, and in the course of the improvements the old Tudor town hall of 1558, built over the bridge-end, was swept away and a new town hall (the present one) was built with help from the Cecils. Several of the town gates were removed — St Peter's gate about 1770, St Paul's gate about 1780, Scotgate in 1780 'owing to its ruinous and dangerous condition', and St George's gate (last repaired in 1757) in 1806. Within the town, markets and fairs were re-located to ease the flow of traffic. The shambles in High Street near St Michael's church were rebuilt in 1751, and in 1795 the Monday market cross in Broad Street was removed and the area covered in. It was around these markets — the corn market at the cross in Broad Street, the leather, beast and hay markets also in Broad Street, the sheepmarket, with whitemeat and butter markets in Red Lion Square, the whitemeat market and the shambles in High Street, the market around St Mary's church — that the town's social and economic life centred.

But not all the people, of course, were prosperous. Poverty concerned both the corporation and the individual throughout the century, especially as poor rates escalated (£35 in 1706, £37 in 1760, £147 in 1770, and £264 in 1784). Four privately endowed hospitals (almshouses) had been established by the early years of the eighteenth century in the town. The corporation founded (and for a short time supported) a Spinning School in the recently rebuilt Brazenose (alongside the present Brazenose House) 'for employing the poor of this town' in 1704 — 'in which a great many poor Children have been since constantly employ'd in Spinning, and withal taught to read and instructed in Religion, Psalmody, writing, etc., as far as the circumstances of the children and school will admit . . .'; but in 1734 this became the town workhouse (for all parishes except St Mary's) and the school was transferred to the north side of St Paul's Street. The Bluecoat School, founded by private subscription in 1704, was part of this charitable effort. Later (1794-6), the town council built a series of sixteen single-room back-to-back houses in Scotgate (Corporation Buildings) to lease cheaply to the poor. The process of building rows of tenements to the rear of street-front houses (perhaps beginning in about 1749 in St Leonard Street) had progressed substantially by the end of the century.

Like most towns of the period, Stamford was surrounded by its poorer quarters. St Paul's Street was one area of meaner housing; so too was the area around St George's gate. The main centre, however, was in Scotgate. Disastrous fires decimated the area on several occasions, notably in 1726, and the borough council strengthened its fire services and sued out 'briefs' (the equivalent of the modern 'Appeal') from the Lord Chancellor to raise funds in the face of disasters. The desire for segregation of the respectable classes within the town grew; concern over cleansing and paving the streets, expressed most strongly in 1695 when the council ordered that, in preparation for the visit of William III, 'all the dust and rubbish in the severall streets within the Corporation be swept up and carried away before nine of the clock on Monday next morning . . .', was reiterated time and again. In 1782, the sheep market was removed from Barn Hill to the castle area on the complaint of some of the residents there. But as time went on and population increased (in 1785 it was estimated a total of some 3,800 persons lived in Stamford; by 1801 this total had reached 4,022) it was impossible to keep distinct those areas where rich and poor lived. The presence of the town's open fields, not available for new building, prevented an outward expansion except along Scotgate, and thus it was that Harrod wrote in 1785: 'there are none such [ie void sites] in this parish [St Michael] now, nor indeed in any other . . . many useless shabby places which have been built and let for treble the sum, not to mention the erections without the town towards the north'. The newly furbished face of Georgian Stamford had come, by the end of the eighteenth century, to hide an unacceptable level of congestion.

St Paul's Street, before the widening of Star Lane.

All Saints Place: fully developed Georgian style.

ABOVE: Cottages affected by new style: the house with the bays in the middle of this range is dated 1662; the one to the left is dated 1685. The cross wing on the corner has a mediaeval roof. BELOW: Georgian houses in St Mary's Street.

OPPOSITE LEFT: Georgian houses in St Paul's Street, south and RIGHT: St Mary's Place; BELOW: the Theatre, St Mary's Street; ABOVE: the Town Hall built in a more restrained style towards the end of the eighteenth century; BELOW: Assembly Rooms in St George's Square.

TOLLS TO BE TAKEN AT THIS BRIDGE

	L.	s.	d.
For every laden waggon (*Passing or Repassing*) the sum of	—	—	4
For every laden cart ... D⁰	—	—	2
For every Horse laden or led ... D⁰	—	—	0½
For every Stone Horse ... D⁰	—	—	1
For every score of Beast ... D⁰	—	—	4
All Beasts under five ... D⁰ *each*	—	—	0¼
For every score of cows & calves ... D⁰	—	—	8
For every score of Hogs ... D⁰	—	—	8
For every score of Sheep ... D⁰	—	—	2
For every pair of Millstones ... D⁰	—	—	6

STAMFORD and KETTERING TURNPIKE-ROAD.—*TOLLS to be LET.*

NOTICE is hereby given, that the TOLLS arising at the several Toll-gates, called the EASTON GATE and SIDE GATE, the DUDDINGTON GATE, the WELDON GATE, and the KETTERING GATE, upon the Turnpike-road leading from Saint Martin's, Stamford Baron, to Kettering, in the county of Northampton, will be LET by AUCTION, to the best bidder, at the KING'S ARMS INN in WELDON, in the said county, on WEDNESDAY the 24th day of AUGUST next, between the hours of Eleven o'clock in the Forenoon and Three in the Afternoon, in manner directed by the Act passed in the third and fourth years of the reign of his late Majesty King George the Fourth, "for regulating Turnpike-roads," for such term and under such conditions as the Trustees shall think fit, and to commence from the 11th day of OCTOBER next; which Tolls were let for and produced the last year the sums hereinafter mentioned above the expenses of collecting them, and will be put up at those sums respectively: viz.

        The Easton Gate and Side Gate £350
        The Duddington Gate 144
        The Weldon Gate 155
        The Kettering Gate 330

Whoever happens to be the best bidder, must at the

OPPOSITE: Heavy Georgian ornament: ABOVE: on a new house, Barn Hill. LEFT; on the facade of an older house, St George's Square. RIGHT: End of century finesse: Stamford Hotel Mews. ABOVE: Trade was a source of profit: tolls on the bridge and BELOW: on the turnpike roads.

THESE are to give Notice, That SAMUEL LANE, who kept the Talbot Inn at Peterborough in Northamptonshire, is lately Removed to the White Swan (the Post-Office) in Stamford, Lincolnshire, where Gentlemen, &c. may be well accommodated, with good Usage.

Inns: ABOVE: the George Hotel. This drawing shows the building as it was before the Georgian dining room was added and Station Road demolished the buildings on the right; LEFT: White Swan Hotel in St Mary's Street; RIGHT: poor relief in St George's parish register.

ABOVE: The Callis on St Peter's Hill (before restoration). BELOW:
One of a new series of almshouses. Fryer's Hospital.

LEFT: Memorial tablet of the founder of Truesdale's Hospital.
Stamford Free Grammar School in St Paul's church. BELOW: exterior.
RIGHT: Interior.

The Future Ends, The Past Begins

'The old busy air, since the introduction of railways,
is also missing; and the constant passages of coaches,
carriages with postilions and outriders and horsemen,
along the Great North Road, no longer enlivens its
quiet streets; but the comparative calm better suits
their antique look, so unlike the pretentious primness
and dull uniformity of more bustling and modern towns,
and renders them far more attractive to the
Archaeologist'.

Walcott, 1888

Stamford went to pieces in the nineteenth century; the most conspicuous growth point was in nostalgia.

A clear example of this is the debate in the early years of the century over the Navigation. Alarmed about falling trade and lost opportunities, the leading citizens looked to the canal movement and the profits it had brought to other neighbouring towns such as Grantham with its new link to the Trent at Nottingham. Various schemes were mooted — to build a canal from Oakham through Stamford and across the newly drained fens to Boston, a project devised as early as 1786 and promoted in 1792 and again in 1810; or to link Stamford to the Trent and thus to Nottingham; or to join the Welland to Market Harborough and thence into the Grand Junction Canal. But the issue became bedevilled by the electoral opposition to the Cecil family; indeed it was asserted that all plans were 'strenuously opposed' by the corporation and other adherents of the Earl of Exeter, and in the end nothing was done. Stamford came to the point too late. The river below the bridge continued to carry some light traffic until 1863 (the corporation sold its interests in the Navigation a few years later), but above the bridge it was the mills which dominated the waterline.

Stamford also missed the railway; as everyone knows, the Great Northern Railway line from London passed through Peterborough and not through Stamford on its way to Grantham and the North. The decision in 1844 to take this route was vital to the town's development, and the Act of 1845 was greeted in Stamford with ringing of the church bells. It is no longer clear that the Earl of Exeter actively opposed the building of the line through Stamford, and the reasons for the decision seem to have lain outside of the town, not inside, with Earl Fitzwilliam lobbying Parliament on behalf of Peterborough with great success. Links with the new line were provided, first by the Syston and Peterborough line in 1846 (the second line to be built in any Lincolnshire town) which was extended two years later to Melton Mowbray and Leicester to the west, and secondly (1856) by the Stamford and Essendine Branch Railway; both stations were built south of the river on land made available by the Exeter estate. A proposed link to Wisbech was however abandoned. Such lines made possible the greater mobility of the inhabitants of Stamford, and a link with the east coast for holidays seems to have been forged; but they probably brought little trading benefit to a declining town. Indeed the daily number of mail and stage coaches which passed through the town (more than seventy in the 1830s) declined sharply after the stations were opened. During the early years of the century, the turnpike roads around Stamford were the busiest in the region, yielding more tolls (over £4,000 pa) even than the roads around Lincoln; but they declined from a peak in the 1830s in the face of rivalry from the railways.

The fairs and markets of the town thus kept up well for a time during the first half of the nineteenth century, for the town continued to serve a wide region in at least four neighbouring counties. *The Lincoln, Rutland and Stamford Mercury* (a 'liberal' paper outside the borough of Stamford, where it more regularly supported church and state) was the first newspaper for Lincolnshire and region; attempts to found such a paper in Lincoln in 1728, 1744, 1785, and 1809 all failed. A series of attempts to establish papers in Boston (1810) and elsewhere in the county, especially during the crisis years of the reform agitation, 1828-34, were equally unsuccessful, but from 1836 more success attended efforts to establish a Lincoln-based regional newspaper. The *Mercury,* however, continued to provide an advertisement service for the farmers and tradesmen of a large area, but Stamford's changing relations with its neighbours are illustrated by the career of the *Lincolnshire Chronicle,* established in the town in 1833 and in 1850 bought up and moved to Lincoln.

The town was still a focal point for trade and remained so, despite the disastrous years at the end of the Napoleonic Wars when at least two of the town's banks collapsed (1814-15). In 1821 it was reported that there had been an increase in wool, sheep and horses sold in the Stamford fairs. The main fair was the Mid-Lent one, but other fairs were still held in February, May, June, August and November. There was some disorder at these gatherings but, on the whole, they were still events of significance and prosperity until the second half of the century when they declined.

The markets however seem to have declined rather earlier. The whitemeat market in Red Lion Square and the Monday market in St Mary's Place were moved to 'the Covered Part at the South End of the NEW MARKET' (the present Public Library) in High Street in 1808 — a building which also housed the town beadle, fire engine and police offices. The corn market in Broad Street flourished for a while — in 1819, it was the fourth largest outside London; but by the time a new structure was built for it in front of Browne's Hospital in 1839, it was already in decline, and the Corn Exchange erected in 1859 was excessively grand for the size of the market by that date. The arches from the dismantled earlier market were sold and scattered about the town. The cattle market remained in Broad Street until the very end of the century. A new butter market was built in Red Lion Square in 1861 but for a time it was housed in the Portico or 'New Market' in High Street.

The architecture of Stamford during the nineteenth century shows this lack of cohesion and self-confidence. Although in 1822 it was said that the town had 'of late years . . . been much improved by new buildings', this did not continue. There were few men of note leaving their mark on the town. Among the best were the Brownings, father and son, but even their style was not distinctive. Despite work which spread throughout the town, they did not stamp their character on Stamford in the way that Hine and Fothergill Watson, for instance, did on Nottingham, and other architects did on other Victorian towns. Outsiders were called in on occasion, like George Basevi (the hospitals) or John Gandy (the Infirmary) or J. L. Bond (Stamford Hotel) or James Fowler from Louth (Browne's Hospital). Nineteenth century work in Stamford is a hotch-potch and derivative; it has nothing of the assertiveness and assurance that characterise building in other towns in this period.

One reason for this may have been the crowded nature of the town and the small sites available for building throughout the century. Only one large area inside the town walls was comprehensively redeveloped — Castle Street — and the opportunity there was lost. Rows of artisan housing were built on one side of the widened road, small commercial premises on the other side. Rutland Terrace, on the bowling green outside the west gate, was the major achievement of the century, twenty houses built between 1827 and 1831; but a plan by John Cust, newly created Earl Brownlow (Lord-lieutenant of the county and a long-standing landholder in Stamford) to build a new estate at Blackfriars to the south-east of the town (1840-44) foundered unsuccessfully. South of the river the Exeter estate laid out the Church Street area in the 1820s and 1830s, but much of the land enclosed in 1796 was incorporated into Burghley Park and not released for building. At the top of St Mary's Hill, a grand scheme to link St Mary's Street and High Street with an ornate parade of shops in 1848-9 came to nothing. The new road laid out to the south of the river to link the bridge to the railway station was never fully developed; although wide and flanked by trees, the buildings along it did nothing to enhance the approach to the town. Around the town some attempt was made to create an immediate impression — the so-called Bottle Lodges of 1799 to the south, part of the new layout to Burghley Park, the new bridge and its buildings (Conservative Club, toll house, etc) built by the Brownings in 1849, and to the north, Rock House and Rock Terrace, Richard Newcomb's work in 1841-2. Later in the century the two public schools, Stamford School, rebuilt and extended in 1833, and the High School in St Martin's, founded in 1875, added distinction to the town.

The town became more and more congested. Population rose from 4,000 in 1801 north of the river and just over 1,000 south of it to 9,000 in 1851 to the north and nearly 1,800 to the south. Like the surrounding rural areas, Stamford's population reached a peak in 1851; thereafter population fell — to just over 8,000 for both parts of the town in 1861. The growth rate in the early part of the century — from 5,000 to nearly 11,000 between 1801 and 1851 — was impressive. It was of course much smaller than that of many other towns at the same period: Nottingham, for instance, trebled itself from 1801 (9,000) to 1851 (27,000). But it was still substantial for a small town, about the same as that for nearby Grantham (4,300 in 1801 to 10,800 in 1851). But by 1861, the 'rural' nature of Stamford came to predominate; at a time when other towns continued to expand, Stamford contracted.

Despite this doubling of population in the first fifty years of the nineteenth century, the built-up area of the town hardly expanded at all. To the north lay the unenclosed town fields; to the west lay the meadows; while to the east lay the sites of two former friaries and St Leonard's priory, all owned by great landlords. To the south lay Burghley Park, extended in 1796. Land for building was thus restricted. The town fields were no longer open in fact; they were divided up among the farmers who cultivated the plots in severalty, and the farmsteads lay within the town. Disputes between the tenants over the removal of 'the land-mark showing the boundary of [their] take' had become 'a too common practice in the field' (1843), and the fieldreeve and the tithingman were called in to settle such matters. What prevented the use of this land for building was the inability of the town council, the surviving freemen and the lord of the manor (the Earl of Exeter, newly created Marquis of Exeter) to agree about the ownership of the waste, especially a narrow belt of land immediately to the north of the town on which had been built a considerable number of slum cottages (nearly 400 by 1845). It was an undesirable area, home of thieves and prostitutes; but the ownership of the land and the disposal of the freehold right to the three hundred or so houses which existed by 1869 was a matter of moment to the contending parties. Both sides attempted (unsuccessfully) to collect rent or fines and to eject occupiers for non-payment. When eventually agreement was reached, the Exeter estate asserted its right to a broad belt of land immediately around the town. Quarrels like this delayed the enclosure of Stamford's open fields until 1870 (the Enclosure Act) and even 1875 (the Enclosure Award).

The Exeter relationship with the borough during the nineteenth century was a complicated one. It had at least three main aspects. First, the Exeter family were landlords of a substantial part of the town. From this property they drew a good deal of income; and their concern was expressed in the provision of various services for the town, notably the waterworks which belonged to the Exeter estate and for which a separate rate was levied by the lord's agent. Secondly, and not of course unassociated with the former, he was *de facto* the planning authority, and his interests ranged from the development of new industries and new means of communication to the preservation of vistas and antiquities. On occasion, his power was used to try to prevent change. The Municipal Corporation Commission of 1832 reported that his influence 'is exercised to check the natural progress of improvement'; but at other times he led the provision of amenities. Thirdly, he was political master of a town which (until 1867) returned two Members of Parliament and from then until 1885 one Member of Parliament.

The Exeter interest, arising, as it did, 'from three causes — viz. his property, his employment of tradesmen, and his visiting and entertaining the gentry', was exercised in many different aspects of the life of the town. His servants controlled most fields of local government. The estate's agent Jeremiah Clapton was also registrar of births, marriages and deaths after the 1836 Civil Registration Act. He was clerk to the Board of Guardians of the Poor Law Union which was set up in 1835 (Lord Exeter being the first chairman) and later clerk to the local Burial Board. In addition he was the agent of the local branch of the Conservative Party. The ear of the Cecils' agent was needed if one wished to obtain a place in one of the town's almshouses, or in the grammar school or one of the town's church benefices.

Such control did not mean that the Marquis of Exeter's political will was always meekly accepted by the town. Indeed, the lengths to which he had to go in order to secure the return of his candidates as Members of Parliament for Stamford shows the strength of the opposition. When the tithe commissioners of 1839 compared Lord Exeter's control of Stamford to 'a state of barbarous intervention and blindness which resembles more an African domination than an English and wholesome interference', they were exaggerating; so too were those who on the other side propounded the view that in 1831 the town held the reputation of staging 'the greatest battle between the aristocracy and the people'. A radical streak persisted in Stamford throughout most of the century, and it is not without significance that Robert Owen, the reformer, served his draper's apprenticeship in the town. Much of the opposition to the Cecil sway centred round the *Stamford Mercury* or other newspapers in the town. John Drakard, drawing upon the experience of Harrod's radical paper the *Stamford Herald* (later the *Loyal Intelligencer*) 1793-97, published the *Stamford News* from 1809 to 1834 (like the *Mercury,* a weekly appearing each Friday) and for a few years another weekly (on Tuesdays) called the *Stamford Champion* (1830-33) which carried a banner 'Priced at 3d. and tax (to prevent the poor from reading) 4d.'. His libellous attacks on many of the nobility, especially members of the Cecil family, landed him in court and even in prison, and at least one nobleman sought to horsewhip him for statements that appeared in his paper. He attacked equally 'the passive, not to say servile, mind of the late and present generations of its inhabitants (who suffer themselves to be held completely under the domination of the house of Burghley)', contrasting it in a way characteristic of Stamford's use of history with 'the vigour and firmness of their forefathers'. 'Between the domineering and arbitrary influence on the one hand and the pusillanimous and subservient conduct on the other, there appears but little hope of the town's improvement.' Drakard's vituperous cause was taken up, but with differences, by Richard Newcomb.

It was at the parliamentary elections that the greatest opposition to Cecil control was expressed. The 1801 election, when General Bertie was one of the successful candidates, passed off quietly, but in 1809 things were different; the Cecil nomination, uncontested since 1734 faced its first serious challenge. The 'Blews' and the Reds emerged, the Reds centred on the George Hotel in St Martin's where Exeter had the greatest influence, and the Blews (sponsored in 1809 by the Noel family of Exton who led the opposition to Exeter) using the George and Angel for their headquarters. The Noels contested the elections twice, in 1809 and 1812. In 1809 they set in hand the building of the pretentious Stamford Hotel (or the New Hotel, as it was first called) next to the George and Angel as the headquarters of their election committee, 'an extensive building of which' (it was said) 'in a town life Stamford, no possible use can be made' (perhaps a reference to the fact that it seems to have stood empty until about 1825). The Noels and the candidate they sponsored in 1809 (J. J. Oddy, a visiting 'merchant of great eminence'), supported as they were by two of the town's bankers and the owner of the silk throwing mills, also built eighteen houses in Scotgate and called them 'Protection Place' as they were intended to house those Cecil tenants evicted from their rented homes for not voting in accordance with the Cecil mandate; Oddy erected more such dwellings off High Street (Billings Buildings). Riots and disorder accompanied the election then and three years later in 1812 (when a duel was fought between Richard Newcomb and Octavius Gilchrist over Newcomb's remarks about Gilchrist's behaviour during the election). In 1818, for lack of local candidates willing to oppose the Exeter interests, two 'esquires . . ., merely passing through Stamford on business, were detained at the solicitation of a few of the electors', but the issue came to nothing. Disorder (not always related to elections) broke out again in 1828 and 1830. The Noels withdrew by 1831, to be replaced by the Tennyson family, but riots continued. And the pressure succeeded at last; for the first time for almost exactly one hundred years, one of the Cecil candidates was defeated. In 1832 both the George and Angel (the headquarters of the Blews) and the next door property, the Stamford (or Standwell's as it was then) Hotel, at that time anachronistically the headquarters of the Reds, were attacked by the mob. In 1832, St Martin's parish was included within the parliamentary boundaries of the borough by the Reform Act, and the former 'scot and lot' franchise was abolished in favour of the £10 householder, thus reducing the number of voters. Sir Charles Tennyson (who had won against great odds in 1831) decided that he could no longer fight against the increased weight that this piece of legislation gave to the Exeter interest, and withdrew, leaving Stamford (along with Grantham) as the only place in the country to return Tories to the new parliament.

Contested elections continued, however, with Richard Newcomb, son of a printer from Uppingham who came to Stamford in 1784, taking over the *Mercury* about 1830, becoming leader of the opposition. Newcomb followed in the pattern set by the Custs and later the Noels. He bought up both the George and Angel (1843) and Standwell's Hotel (1845) from the Noels and set up his own scheme to improve the appearance of the town. He built houses along Scotgate, notably Rock Terrace (1841-44) and Rock House (1842) on the site of a quarry purchased from the Drakard family, and other houses behind them. But he was not able to succeed where others had failed. From 1847 to 1874 the borough elections went uncontested and the Cecil control lasted until the death of the second Marquis in 1867, at the same time as the new Reform Act abolished one of Stamford's seats in parliament and just prior to the introduction of the secret ballot in 1872, which would have rendered such manipulation impossible. It was nearly but not quite true that Stamford, as Gladstone put it, had for forty years or so returned at Lord Exeter's behest some 'wandering Tory official who had been rejected by some constituency that was weary of him'; nor was it quite true, as the Reform League reported in 1868, that 'For years past Stamford has been a pocket borough belonging to the Marquis of Exeter . . . there is no independence in the place'. But it is true that the Cecils fought and won so that in the end it could be said that 'Everything in the shape of a Liberal organization has completely died out'. It is therefore anachronistic that, after the death of the second Marquis, the last MP for the town (1880-1885) was a Liberal.

Stamford then was not, as Oddy put it in 1809, completely 'reduced . . . to the degrading situation of a pocket borough'; the Cecils had to fight hard to win in each contested election. But contesting a Stamford seat was costly, both in financial and personal terms. The wooing of the electorate was rough and involved corruption by all sides on a large scale. The reputation of the town attracted a parliamentary committee of inquiry and at least one delegation of observers from overseas. In the process the nobility of the neighbourhood was attracted to the town; the Tennyson family for instance put up its coat of arms over the front of the George and Angel in 1831 prior to the election. The balls, races and theatre in the town were still fashionable, patronised by the gentry of Lincolnshire, Rutland, Northamptonshire and Leicestershire.

But the nobility no longer found in Stamford a pleasant place in which to make their homes. They were not prepared to build town houses there for themselves. The discovery of mineral springs in the Meadows and the building of a small spa was a half-hearted attempt to engrace the town. Exeter did make some efforts to beautify the place; his rebuilding scheme (1849) at the north of the bridge, with inn, toll house and Conservative Club together presenting a unified entrance to the town, was intended to impress as well as to express his control. But the over-crowding generated by the growth of population and the failure to provide new building land by enclosure of the town's open fields, together with the congestion created by the heavy road traffic (a scheme for the Great North Road to by-pass the town in 1830 was defeated) made Stamford more and more undesirable as a place in which to live. The slums surrounding the town, the over-built courtyards inside the walls, the markets with their noise, smell and disorder on at least three days a week — all these represented a supposed loss of 'gentility' from the eighteenth century. The lack of lighting and paving 'and the general prevalence of filth in the streets, more particularly in those of the outskirts' were causes of frequent complaint.

The borough council too was weakened. In 1835 the Muncipal Corporations Act deprived the traditional freemen of most of their powers and left them merely to manage their own property. A new council of eighteen members (and six aldermen) was established but it received few powers; responsibility for town amenities passed to a separate group of Improvement Commissioners who operated between 1841 and 1870. There was a certain amount of road-widening and some new developments (as on the corner of Red Lion Square and High Street in 1846-8), and a municipal cemetery to replace the small congested churchyard burial grounds was provided in 1855 under the general Burial Act of two years earlier. Little more was done; and the concerns of the new authorities were the same as the old — minor matters such as paving, lighting, refuse disposal and law and order. Gas was provided by a private company under a separate Act of Parliament of 1823, and water from Lord Exeter's waterworks at Wothorpe from 1837.

Nevertheless Stamford corporation was well served during the century by a series of loyal and able town clerks drawn from among the most influential of the lawyers of the town. John Wyche directed the town's affairs for fifty years (1770-1820). His place as town clerk was taken by Jeremiah Clapton, Lord Exeter's political agent, as a means towards reducing friction. James Torkington defended the interests of the borough against what he saw as encroachments by Lord Exeter's interests. Joseph Phillips took over as clerk to the Board of Guardians (he later became the first clerk to the new Lincolnshire County Council), and from 1861 three members of the Atter family held the post of town clerk for the next seventy or so years.

Some attempts were made to increase the grace and the amenities of the town. St Michael's church in the High Street (which in 1808 housed the only organ in the town) fell down during restoration in 1832 and was rebuilt in the new style with gallery and elaborate pewing. Apart from new pews, the other mediaeval churches were left untouched, and no attempt was made by them to reach the unchurched of the town. The Congregational Chapel in Star Lane was rebuilt in 1819 on a large scale to reflect its increasing respectability, while the Roman Catholic congregation moved from humble premises in All Saints Street to Broad Street, where the new chapel was opened in 1865. The Methodists, arriving relatively late on the scene (1800), displayed their sensibilities and the character of their support in the town by building their chapel in Barn Hill, among the houses of the prosperous. Only one group apparently made any attempt to reach the poor; two Baptist chapels were opened within a year of each other, both among the cottages of the encroachment, one in Bath Row and the other (supported by a local doctor, J. G. de Merveilleux) in North Street (1834-5).

The two large new Anglican vicarages built for St George's church (1881) and All Saints church show how far these churches were distancing their officiants from their flocks.

Schools too continued to abound all over the town. Private schools were held in various houses and their attractions advertised regularly. Apart from Radcliffe's Free Grammar School and the Bluecoat School (for a time affiliated to the British and Foreign Schools Society), parts of various charities (including Browne's Hospital estate) were used to provide free education for the poor of the town. A Sunday School had been opened in All Saints parish as early as 1785, and by 1816 the Methodists had opened their own. The first National (parish) School was opened in the town in 1815 (St George's parish, for girls), and this and the Wells Petty School which served All Saints parish were matched in other parishes: thus new ones were opened during the century (St John's parish school, an 'Infants School' in North Street, and St Martin's, based on the earlier Cecil school in that parish). The involvement of the Church of England in the education of Stamford's children meant that in 1870 a School Board was not needed for the town, and the tradition of voluntary schooling has continued to this day.

All of this was part of an attempt to enforce gentility on the town. One focus of this campaign was on the bull-running, 'this plebeian carnival' as it was called in 1807; attempts were made time and again to secure the abolition of this customary and brutal sport which took place each November and at other times. As early as 1788-90, the practice was banned; in 1828, the government sent in the troops (the Third Dragoons from Northampton) to reinforce the police but they were foiled: 'stones were thrown at the police and some severe blows were given and received'. The final run seems to have taken place in 1839 when, in scenes of disorder between populace, the Fifth Dragoons and a force of metropolitan police, the last of the Stamford bulls was 'arrested' and escorted out of the town.

Other attacks on what had come to be called 'the present culture' were made throughout the century. The disorders at the fairs which on occasion (as for instance in 1855) caused troops to be stationed in the town led to calls for their abolition; and in 1830 the Duke of Richmond's 'Sussex Plan', whereby a constabulary was enlisted from 'yeomen, shop-keepers and respectable labourers', was put into force in Stamford. In 1821, a new gaol was opened.

But 'gentility' needed more than the enforcement of restrictive laws if it was to be effective. A new hospital for twelve in-patients, provided by public subscription, was built in 1825-8 on the site of one of the earlier friaries to the east of the town walls. The gasworks built in 1825 to the south-east of the town, between the walls and the river, provided street lights for greater security and formed a focus for the development of a small industrial area. The town provided itself with some of the amenities of a self-respecting urban community, such as the Stamford Institution 'for the dissemination of literary, philosophical, scientific, mechanical and other useful knowledge' (1838) in Broad Street, moving in 1842 to its St Peter's Hill premises with concert and lecture hall, museum, library and reading room, and later a camera obscura (photography was an early hobby in the town); a reaction by 'the humbler classes of the town' against the 'patronage' which they perceived in this Institution led to the establishment of a rival Mechanics Institute in 1841. The town still had to be worthy of the visits of Royalty (Queen Adelaide came in 1842 and Queen Victoria later) and of the noble house parties which Lord Exeter held from time to time (Barn Hill House was altered in 1844 to accommodate the Marquis's guests).

This pre-occupation with gentility prevented the full flowering of industry in Stamford. Unlike Grantham or other neighbouring towns, Stamford never developed a strong industrial base; the range of occupations was still wide and of a service nature — quill makers, pipe makers, soap makers, clockmakers (several well known craftsmen like John Wilson were at work in the town) and coachmakers, for example. The existing iron foundries in the town were reinforced by one to the north of the town in 1771 and others in the nineteenth century, but they never developed into a full agricultural engineering industry as elsewhere. All (except Blackstones) were on a small scale, like the foundry at the north end of Star Lane; their location within the walls of the old town reflected their lack of expansion. The most important, Ashby and Jeffrey, later Blackstones, began in the Sheepmarket near the castle in 1837 and moved twice before settling down in Foundry Road in 1842; the firm developed a new — but unsuccessful — traction engine in the 1870s. The Marquis of Exeter in 1845 established a new foundry in Wharf Road near the Gas Works leased to J. C. Grant, 'agricultural implement maker and brass founder', but later in 1859 this became the terracotta works of J. N. Blashfield, who moved into Stamford from London, making ornaments and paving tiles for houses and churches. Another terracotta works, run by Henry Lumby, stood in High Street St Martin's, and a sacking factory in Barn Hill. When the steam engine boom hit the agricultural areas, Stamford lagged far behind the other major towns in the county, each of which held four or more firms producing the new machines; along with smaller towns and villages like Kirton Lindsey, Welby near Grantham and Brigg, the town only had one such firm (Smith and Ashby), a sign of its reluctant industrialisation — and an opportunity which nearby Peterborough seized. The lament of a visitor in 1789, 'Stamford is a large, but an ill-built town, without shade around it or manufactory within it', bears witness both to the prejudice of the writer and to Stamford's tradition of gentility and trade rather than industry. Whether this was because, as was alleged by Thomas Blore early in the century, the town was 'totally subservient to the control of a neighbouring nobleman [to such an extent that its residents were] destitute of that energy and spirit in commercial and manufacturing speculations for which those that have emancipated themselves shine forth', may still be a point of argument.

The name of Lumby, however, is most closely connected with one of Stamford's more successful industries — milling, malting and brewing. Stamford's mills, both the watermills on the Welland and the windmills on the ridge above the town, were of great antiquity and well supported; the House of Commons was told in 1847 that more than 2,500 bushels of corn were ground in the town every week. Malting too was prominent, drawing upon the barley of the surrounding region. Moses Lumby, a butcher, built his maltings and a twin row of cottages to house his workers south of the river, while Phipps not only brewed, but bought up public houses in which to sell his products. In 1825, a 'New Brewery' had been founded on a site between Scotgate and All Saints Street, near to that used as early as 1700 as a 'Malting Office' by William Truesdale. Here it was that poor Elizabeth Pollard, aged 69, was 'suffocated in a Porter cask' in 1832. By 1872 it had become Melbourn's and developed an early form of Patent Steam brewing. Various forms of drinks — both 'soft' and alcoholic — were made in the town: but some were stronger than mineral waters. Justin Simpson referred to Harvey's Ginger Beer as 'an article much in request and being well made commanded a brisk trade long before the advent of aerated waters; it was "real stingo" and different to such as is sold under the same name'. But once again the industry never flourished; as late as 1880, there were still at least fifteen 'Publican-brewers' in the town, brewing their own beer for consumption in their own licensed premises, despite the five 'common-brewers' who were beginning to acquire 'tied houses' throughout Stamford. Stamford thus did not develop into a town like Newark, at once a railway junction, agricultural engineering manufactory and malting centre.

The textile industry of Stamford was reflected in the nineteenth century by a continuation of silk weaving, following perhaps the tradition of the silk spinning school of a century earlier. In 1785, the spinning 'school' had forty children and thirty women employed in it, and in all some 500 persons in the town were engaged in silk working in a local factory and other branches of the industry. New silk mills were established in 1803 'principally for throwing of Organizing Silk'; they were leased as a going concern in 1815 and, by 1836, when they were described as a silk winding factory 'in the fields to the north of the town', they were being used for linen manufacture. Various attempts were made at developing the textile industry in the town — George Gouger's steam-powered silk mills in 1816, or damask weaving, or Nottingham lace-making in the 1820s, or Mrs Knight's linen factory in 1836 — were all however short-lived.

A rough survey of the occupations in the town in 1851, made by the Stamford Survey Group, shows a remarkably evenly balanced economy without any predominating interests. The groups engaged in agriculture, in building, in working in wood or in leather, in textiles, in victualling, in professional occupations, and in the thriving hostelry service were almost exactly equal; smaller groups of brewers, metalworkers, merchants and printers followed. The servant population was small, very small for a town of this character, while the number of those of 'independent means' was high. As one writer put it, Stamford in 1851 was 'a hard-working and productive community, principally inhabited by those who worked with their hands for a local market'. Everything was on a small scale.

Since industry on a large scale did not exist in nineteenth century Stamford, working class housing was not provided on a large scale. There was of course some. Early in the nineteenth century yards such as the sixteen houses in Exeter Court off St Peter's Street filled up many narrow tenements and back yards, occupied by working class families. About thirty-six units for artisans were built by the Exeter estate south of Castle Street on the model of Glasgow tenements (called Mechanics Buildings). Newcomb built Rock Terrace in the 1840s. During the early years of the century, more cottages were built as encroachments on the manorial wasteland to the north of the town walls, and between the castle and the river (Bath Row); and the lanes south of St Mary's Street became congested with small and mean cottages. New Town sprang up before 1845, the home of small craftsmen and labourers. It was however in the backyards and courts that the independent poor lived, in impoverished and over-crowded conditions. Most have now been cleared away; only a few of the honeycomb of lanes (such as Gas Lane) have survived to show what nineteenth century Stamford was really like.

A report on 'the sanitary state of Stamford in 1870' reveals its condition. The underlying geology, limestone broken up by much building, by quarrying and by natural forces, kept the town surprisingly healthy in view of the fact that only a few streets possessed sewers; the Welland as it passed through the town was 'a most offensive cesspool' and still liable to frequent flooding. Water was supplied from wells in private houses, from the Exeter estate waterworks and from 15 public pumps scattered throughout the town. Severe outbreaks of typhoid, due to polluted water supplies, were recorded in 1868 and 1869.

The condition of the poor was alleviated by the hospitals or poor houses in the town and by the many charitable subscriptions raised in years of dearth. Most of the hospitals were rebuilt or refurbished during the century. Truesdale's (1832) and Snowden's (1822-3), the Callis in All Saints Street (1863) and part of Burghley's Hospital (1849) were reconstructed and a new one (Fryer's) founded. Williamson's Almshouses and Hopkins' Hospital built in 1770 continued to serve the town. Browne's Hospital was plagued with a long, bitter and expensive law-suit in the early years of the century, and this delayed the rebuilding until 1870. Thomas Blore, a local lawyer, set up in 1809 a Society for Reforming Stamford Charity Abuses, and published a tendentious history of the various charities (1813), especially Browne's Hospital, but the trustees weathered the storm and a new scheme was drawn up in 1854; in 1870, a massive programme for 'the re-arranging, re-building and restoring of Browne's hospital' was under way; the inmates were housed in the Daniel Lambert Inn in High Street St Martin's while the work proceeded.

Voluntary help was not enough. In 1834, Stamford became the centre for a large poor law union incorporating a considerable rural area around the town, and a new workhouse was built in 1836 along the Barnack Road in Stamford Baron. It stayed there until 1902 when it was removed to the Bourne Road site. At least five Friendly Societies are known to have existed, meeting in various public houses in the town. But these efforts to deal with Stamford's poor were spasmodic, and it was the enclosure of the town's open fields in the 1870s that brought relief, new housing and new hope to many of the families crowded in the back courts of the congested town.

The congested town: ABOVE: view from St Michael's church southwards
over Stamford Baron; BELOW: St Martin's river edge.

ABOVE: Map of Stamford 1833 by Knipe. BELOW: Rutland Terrace, the only substantial group of houses of this period; it lay just outside the town wall at St Peter's Gate (the fragments of the gate can still be seen).

Nineteenth century streets: OPPOSITE ABOVE: Castle Street (before widening) and St Mary's Street, looking east. ABOVE: St Mary's Street (east). BELOW: Red Lion Street. OPPOSITE BELOW: High Street, St Martin's, as seen by JMW Turner.

St Michael's church, rebuilt in the 1830s. LEFT: Exterior. RIGHT: Mediaeval fragment in 'crypt'. BELOW: Galleried interior.

CONFIRMATION.

The **LORD BISHOP** of **LINCOLN** has given Notice of a Confirmation, to be held at **STAMFORD**, on **WEDNESDAY**, October 25th.

All Residents in St. **GEORGE'S PARISH** who wish to be Confirmed on that occasion are requested to apply to me at the Vestry, in St. George's Church, on Sunday, after Divine Service, September 3rd, 10th, 17th.

In order to avoid the rudeness with which Candidates for Confirmation, meeting at St. George's School Room, have on former occasions been treated by unruly boys, the Confirmation Classes will be held at the Rector's House, 37, St. Martin's.

Henry B. Browning, M.A.,

RECTOR.

August 28th, 1876.

W. H. Mitchell, Printer, Paperhanger, &c., 50, High-street, Stamford.

ONE POUND

REWARD.

SOME DAMAGE HAVING BEEN DONE TO THE

Windows of All Saints' Church,

Stamford, lately (presumably by Catapults), especially on the night of the 13th inst., the above REWARD shall be paid to any person giving such information as will lead to conviction.

HENRY ALLIN,
EDWARD SIMPSON, Churchwardens.

September 14th, 1882.   [HAYNES, PRINTER, STAMFORD.

If the weather be fine, there will be a Church Service in Mr. Edmonds's Garden, on Sunday Morning and Evening next, the 12th of August, at 11 and 6.30 o'clock, to which all in this house are invited to come.

1877

(fine)

Church life: ABOVE: Confirmation at St George's 1876. LEFT: Vandalism 1882. RIGHT: Card invitation to open air service 1877.

ABOVE: Bible Society meeting 1842 (Stamford and Rutland were
regularly linked in the nineteenth century). Notice of: BELOW:
Vestry meeting 1881.

Chapels: ABOVE: Wesleyan Chapel, Barn Hill. LEFT: Congregational
Chapel, Star Lane. RIGHT: St Augustine's RC church, Broad Street.

STAMFORD and RUTLAND INFIRMARY, Tuesday Nov. 4.

IN-PATIENTS.		OUT-PATIENTS.	
Admitted	4	Admitted	10
Discharged	1	Discharged	3
Total number	19	Total number	102

Weekly Visitor, Mr. H. Allin.

ABOVE: Stamford Institution. BELOW: Infirmary: the original buildings; and regular reports were published in the *Stamford Mercury*.

Public services: ABOVE: Bath House; (JD) BELOW: Fire engine.

107

ABOVE: Former offices of *Stamford Mercury* off High Street and now in Sheepmarket. BELOW: Midland Station.

108

Schools: ABOVE: Bluecoat; LEFT: All Saints parish school in Austin Street; RIGHT: Rossi's statue of Justice on the roof of the Stamford Hotel;

ABOVE: Stamford Hotel exterior. BELOW: Horns and Blue Boar, Broad Street.

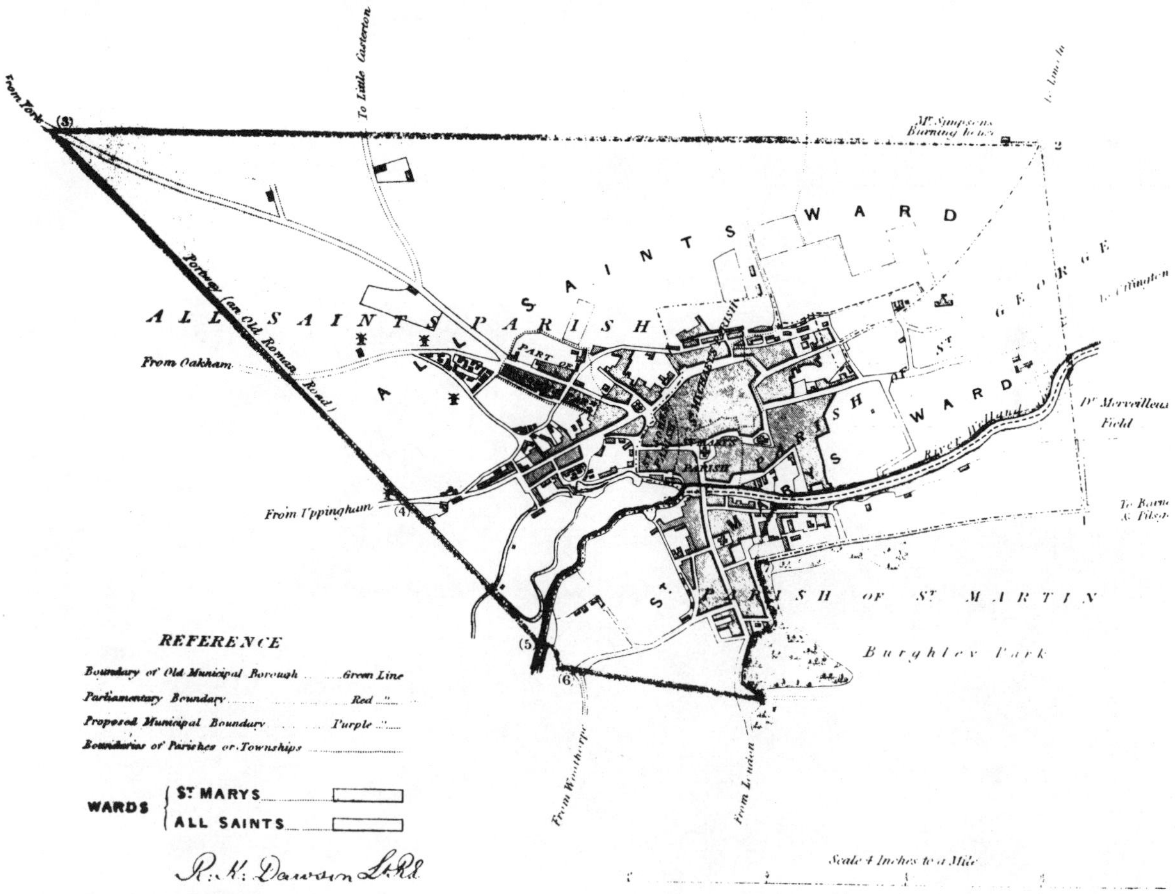

ABOVE: Revised boundaries of Stamford from *Parliamentary Report* 1834.
BELOW: Rock Terrace built by Richard Newcomb as a political gesture.

Cecil beautifies the town: ABOVE: buildings on the north end of the bridge including Conservative Club offices, inn and toll house; BELOW: Bottle Lodges alongside main road into Stamford from the south.

Markets: ABOVE: High Street; BELOW: Portico with market spaces
in front of St Michael's church and at the north end of St George's Street.

113

ABOVE: Red Lion Square. Shops: BELOW: Holkings in Broad Street.

HALL and BROWN respectfully announce to the
ladies of STAMFORD and its vicinity that they have
just received their new Stock adapted to the season:—
Paramatta and Saxony Cloths for Dresses, French and
British Embroidered and Plain Merinos new styles in
Printed Challias, Swiss Satteens, Fancy Twilled Cam-
brics, French Figured Ducapes, new shades in Gros de
Naples, &c. &c.; also a very superior assortment of rich
French Filled Norwich and Thibet Shawls, Embroidered
Thibets, &c.   Their Furs this season are worthy of particular attention, having been purchased to considerable
advantage, and they have consequently been induced to
lay in a very extensive stock.   They have a large assortment of Sable, Chinchilla, Ermine, Lynx, Sable-Minx,
Squirrel, &c. in Muffs, Capes, Pelerines, Mantillas, and
Boas.   Of their permanent Stock of Table Linens, Sheet-
ings, Blankets, Counterpanes, &c., they can speak with
the greatest confidence; their 7-8ths and 4-4ths soft finish
in Irish Linens in particular, ladies having so frequently
expressed their approval of them.   A large stock of Cloaks
on hand, in Silk, Merino, Cloth, and Plaid.

MILLINERY AND DRESS ROOMS.—H. and B. respectfully invite the attention of ladies to their new Fashions
in Millinery, &c., Miss BAMBER having just returned
from London, where she has selected them with particular
care from the most celebrated establishments, and H. & B.
are persuaded that on favoring them with a call ladies
will be more than usually pleased with their variety and
novelty.   Dresses made up in the most fashionable manner.   Models and Patterns of all the newest styles.

Draper's advertisement 1834.

MILLINERY & DRESS ROOMS, *All Saints' Place.*

MESDAMES BAKER respectfully acquaint the nobility, gentry, and ladies of STAMFORD and the Neighbourhood that Miss Baker is now in Town making extensive purchases in Millinery, Cloaks, German, French, and English Velvets, Foreign and British Satins, Watered and Figured Silks, with a variety of fashionable Materials for Morning, Dinner, and Evening Dress, which will be submitted for inspection on THURSDAY, NOVEMBER the 3d, and following days, when the honor of a call will confer an additional favor. *N.B.* French Corsets on the most improved principle.

MILLINERY and DRESS ROOMS, *Barn-hill,*
STAMFORD.

MESDAMES HART and BASSET respectfully announce that their selection of Millinery and Dress Fashions, Cardinals, &c., with which Miss B. has just returned from London, will be submitted for inspection on THURSDAY the 3d of NOVEMBER and subsequent days; when they trust their elegant varieties will meet with the approbation and patronage of their friends.—Mesdames Hart and Basset express their gratitude for the unprecedented favors they have received from the Ladies of STAMFORD and its Vicinity, and trust to share a continuance of those favors they so highly value.   Thursday, Oct. 27th, 1842.

FURS CLEANED and ALTERED, and MOTH
ERADICATED.

J. DIXON, Practical Furrier, impressed with gratitude for an extensive patronage, asks permission of the Ladies of STAMFORD and the Neighbourhood to inform them that the ninth season of his practice has commenced, and all orders entrusted to him will be duly attended to.

Millinery and furrier advertisements 1842.

ABOVE: Shop front in Ironmongers Street. BELOW: Brewing: Simpson's grocery and brewhouse north end of St George's Street.

117

STAMFORD FIELD.
Valuable CROPPING and HORSES.
To be SOLD by AUCTION,
By Mr. RICHARDSON,
On Monday the 1st day of August, 1842,

UPWARDS of Twenty Acres of excellent WHEAT, and Twenty-five Acres of capital BARLEY and OATS, which will be sold in lots ; also Two superior Working MARES, Two capital FILLIES, and an excellent PONY.

The company are requested to meet the auctioneer at Hud's Mills, at One o'clock, and proceed to sale with lot 1, being 5½ Acres of Wheat.

Three months' credit will be given upon approved security, or discount for money.

Stamford, July 21, 1842.

ABOVE: Agriculture: Stamford's fields were still farmed in theory unenclosed until 1872. BELOW: Sheepmarket.

Overcrowding: houses in the back yards: ABOVE LEFT: lane off High
Street; RIGHT: the Olive Branch Hotel, St Leonard's Street (front);
(JSH) RIGHT: the Olive Branch Hotel back yard; (JSH) BELOW
LEFT: houses in Billings Yard, High Street. (JSH)

THE BULL-RUNNING.

Mr. Editor,—I have long contemplated addressing you on two melancholy events which took place at Stamford within the last year: I allude to the accident which happened to the Stamford and Birmingham mail-coach, and the Bull-running. The first was a mere accident; and most providential it was, that it was not attended with more disastrous effects,—for which the inhabitants of Stamford are, no doubt, thankful: the other was the work of man; and, may I not say, it was an evil work?—sure I am that it ought never to be re-acted; and I will add my hearty wishes that it never may.

It was intimated last year that if an attempt had not been made to prevent the bull-running it would not have taken place; and that if the matter were left to itself, it would die a natural death. How perverse are mankind, that a wish in one man to avoid evil and prevent cruelty, should stimulate another to commit both! I have strong reason to believe that no such attempt will be made this year; and I therefore indulge a stronger hope that the intimation given last year will be realised this, and that no bull-running will take place.—It is very true that these cruel diversions have died, and are dying, away; and it is therefore matter of regret that *Stamford*, renowned for its antiquity and learning, should be one of the last places in the kingdom to perpetrate and perpetuate them. They suited ancient times and uncivilised persons, but are a disgrace to Englishmen of the nineteenth century, who boast of the march of intellect.

When I was a boy, there was a bull-baiting at the annual wake or feast in the village where I live. It was held in a place then called the "Bull-Dyke," being part of a moat formerly encompassing a castle which time or the work of man's hand had centuries ago destroyed, so that little of its ruins now remain. This "Bull-Dyke" is now turned to a much better purpose, by being used as a

Bull running complaints, *Stamford Mercury* 1842.

ABOVE: Bull running. (TH) BELOW: The poor: the workhouse.

ABOVE: Artisans' houses in Castle Street, the last of a large tenement development. LEFT: Stamford Bellman. RIGHT: Daniel Lambert, prodigy, died in Stamford 1809.

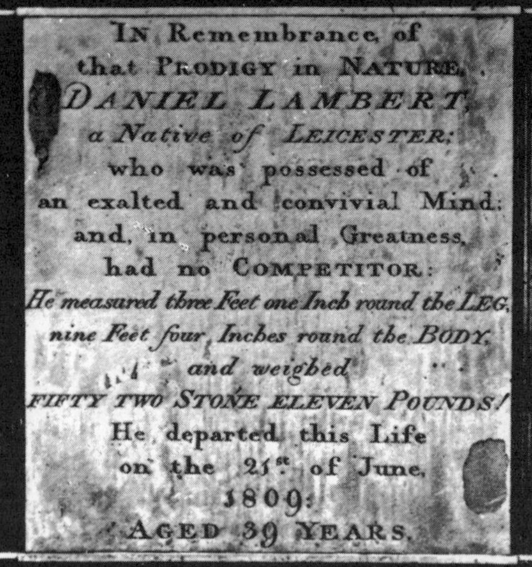

The Modern Town

'The aspect of the town today is one in which the spirit
of medievalism blends with the commercial activity of the
twentieth century, and there are few places in this
county in which the blending is more harmonious'.

Town Guide, 1920

Late in 1869, a momentous meeting was held in the Town Hall. The meeting was held to determine whether there was enough agreement among those with interests, to secure the enclosure of the 1,598 acres of open lands of Stamford. Numerous attempts had been made before but without success; another attempt was now being made. Things were a little different. The second Marquis of Exeter had died in 1867; the town council was a relatively new body; and since 1867 the town had lost one of its two parliamentary representatives. Of the three main bodies involved, the corporation held 83 acres, the freemen as a group (some 57 of them locally resident) held 46 acres and the Exeter estate held 1,100 acres; there were four other private owners (including Mr James Torkington, the town clerk, 'who next to Lord Exeter, was the largest owner of land in the fields') and sixteen public institutions such as Browne's Hospital and most of the parishes.

There were many points at issue. The freemen claimed (and in part had exercised) a traditional right to graze stock on the open fields, and they still grazed the meadows. This right had on at least one occasion landed them in court, and was bitterly disputed by Torkington and others. It was essential, before an Enclosure Award could be made, for a right of common to be established; but if this was done, then all the other holders would suffer, for an allotment would have to be made to the freemen to extinguish any rights that they might or might not have. Secondly there was the problem of building land. 'Nobody would run the risk of building a house on land over which there was a doubtful right of common. The consequence was that in the outskirts there were 300 or 400 houses of the most miserable condition, many without a single inch of ground and without even privy accommodation; and such must continue to be the case unless an inclosure take place . . .'. In the event, however, on this occasion all went well. The Enclosure Act was passed and an Award drawn up and accepted. The Meadows were preserved as common land and allotments made to all the different owners.

One of the forces behind this was clearly the new Lord Exeter. During this episode, it was agreed, 'the Marquis of Exeter had shown a disposition in various ways to improve the town'. It was he who insisted on a Recreation Ground being included in the Award and chose the site himself (Hunt's Close, to the north of the town). He secured for himself as much land as possible close to the town walls so as to preserve a ring of open country near the town — some of which later came to be used by Stamford School and the new Technical College.

Modern Stamford was created by this Act of Parliament. If today the sense of enclosure formerly given by the town walls is gone, it is because that area which was the town until 1872 is now swamped within a larger entity formed mainly of new housing. Building over the newly enclosed land began very quickly but, with population falling, it soon ran out of steam. A string of large houses along the Tinwell Road in the 1880s started the process, but the first large-scale area to be developed was the land between the Bourne Road and the road to Little Casterton. The Freehold Land Society built a whole estate, but mostly the building was done by private speculative developers. Terraces of working class and lower middle class housing spread like a rash across the fields. At the same time, clearance in the inner town area began. Bath Row, North Street and West Street were cleared of their mean cottages, only the most substantial surviving. And within the town walls the opportunity to erect newer and larger premises was not lost; St George's parish built a large new rectory house in St George's Square in 1881, and All Saints parish provided its incumbent with a new parsonage on St Peter's Hill. A borough library was first provided in the early years of the twentieth century. An Oddfellow's Hall was erected in 1876, and a Drill Hall was provided later, 1913. In 1891, the new Kesteven county authority chose Stamford as the site of one of its three Schools of Science and Art in Broad Street. The Grammar School was reconstructed in 1873 and the Girls High School established in 1875.

But this provision of new amenities was local in character, intended for the town rather than the region. Perhaps the loss of Stamford's role as a social centre is symbolised by the turning of the Theatre into a billiard club in 1871. Certainly the town became more inward-looking at this time; and at the same time it became more dependent on outside bodies for services which it had itself formerly provided — thus for instance its own police force, established in the late 1830s, came to an end in 1888.

After the first burst of building came a period of consolidation. From about 1900 to 1920, the town concentrated on cleaning itself up. A new drainage and sewerage system was provided in 1905; a Technical Institute and a public library, both run at town expense, a swimming bath and improved recreation facilities followed. From 1920 onwards, the town responded to government calls to provide council housing. Estates such as the Drift Estate to the north or along Barnack Road to the south of the river were laid out. Progress here was so substantial that by 1961 just over a third of all the houses in the town belonged to the council. Clearance of old property between St Mary's Street and the river and elsewhere in the 'old' town has continued; Lumby's Terrace for instance was partly demolished and restored and Cooch's Court was taken down in the 1950s. More recently the process of expansion over the former open fields has commenced again, but at a slower rate; the Exeter estate to the west or that area of housing known from its street names as 'little Scotland' to the north-west both carry on the tradition set in the 1880s and 1890s. Most of this latest development is private in character. In the town centre, sales of properties by the Exeter estate and others have begun to modify the character of Stamford as predominantly a leasehold town. By the mid-1960s, even the Church of England felt impelled to respond to the new shape of the town; St Michael's in the High Street was closed and Christ Church opened on the Drift Estate. But the rest of the town continues to be served by the town centre churches, all within a few hundred yards of each other.

Despite this rebuilding and a great expansion of the built-up area which covered more than twice the amount of land of the pre-enclosure town, population grew very slowly — from 6,800 in 1861 to 7,200 in 1901; from 9,600 in 1911 (the largest decadal increase since records began in 1801) to 10,000 in 1931 and to under 12,000 in 1961. Population growth here, as elsewhere, did not match housing growth.

The economic basis for this expansion of housing was however weak. Some new industry had been introduced, and two new industrial estates laid out, along the Bourne Road to the north east and (south of the river) on the Barnack Road. The firm of Williamson and Cliffe developed the clay pits at the northern limit of the town's lands into kilns, making a wide range of ceramic wares and bricks, but Woolstone's quarry, established in the town in 1830, ceased to exist by 1916. Blashfield's terracotta works had also come to an end in 1875, and the maltings, one by one, closed from the 1870s onwards. Blackstone's had grown into an international concern with a new oil engine in the 1890's, rivalling Hornsby of Grantham and Ransomes of Ipswich. A range of new products was being created in the town; Hayes and Sons, coach and wagon makers in Scotgate, grew into a major concern, turning out some three hundred new carriage bodies each year in the 1880s; and several models of the Pick car were developed and manufactured in the town, first in Blackfriars Street and later in St Martin's garage, between 1898 and 1925 by J. H. Pick. In addition the town became more clearly a service centre for the region; three rural district councils (set up in 1894) had their headquarters in Stamford — Barnack, Ketton and Uffington (until 1931, when it was abolished).

But the base was still weak and has remained so. One of the railway stations was closed, at a time when road traffic was increasing. The fairs also dwindled; by 1924-5, when foot and mouth disease closed the November stock fairs for a time, there were already complaints about their decline. In 1928 they were moved to a new and less obtrusive site near the surviving railway station (although in 1929 the law was 'flouted' and beasts were sold in Broad Street). As marketing declined and industry failed to develop (or was prevented from developing), so more and more people came to live in Stamford, while working in one of the neighbouring towns. One sign of this smaller role for Stamford was the abolition in 1949 of the town's bench of JPs. Much of the newest building was done in the 1960s when Peterborough was designated a New Town, and it was believed that senior executives would prefer to live among the ancient charms of Stamford rather than in the grimness of the proposed huge new city. The early 1960s were a period of anticipation. Hopes that one of the country's new generation of universities might be established in the town, on the basis of its long traditions, stayed alive for several years — until the student 'troubles' of the late '60s made it seem no longer desirable. Celebrations for the quincentenary of the borough's charters (brought forward a year to coincide with the opening of the long-awaited north-south bypass, in an attempt to keep trade in the town) led to an increased awareness of the town's historic character; and it is no accident that 1965 saw the establishment of the town's Archaeological Research Committee and the Stamford Survey Group to reinforce the older Local History Society (which belonged to Rutland as well as to Stamford) and Stamford's Civic Society (1962). The growth of Stamford was to be on the town's own terms or not at all.

But the early 1960s saw one other event in a long sequence which in the end proved fatal to Stamford. A boundary commission in 1959 proposed that Stamford be moved from Lincolnshire into a new county based on Peterborough. This was of course not the first threat to Stamford in this way. In 1885 a boundary Act had revised the town's limits (removing in the process Stamford's last remaining MP) and, at various stages, suggested revisions to Rutland involved some change in affiliation or status of Stamford. In 1889, when the county councils were established, it was again proposed that Stamford should be incorporated into Rutland; although supported by the town clerk (Charles Atter), it seems to have been opposed by the voters of Rutland on this occasion. During the 1960s debates, all the old arguments for and against the change were made; but it was pointed out strongly that removal from Lincolnshire to another county would solve nothing — Stamford would still remain on the edge of any newly created local authority. An attempt to create a local division with Stamford at the centre, based on the Poor Law parishes incorporated into the Stamford Union, had been made in 1888, but without success. Peripherality was and remained Stamford's greatest problem; in 1885 the town lost its single MP and was merged into a larger, mostly rural constituency.

And in 1974, peripherality proved to be its downfall. At exactly the same moment as the county authorities were reduced in power, so that Stamford's peripheral location no longer mattered so much, the town lost what powers it still possessed. A new boundary commission proposed the creation, in Lincolnshire, of a new series of district councils. And in this matter, as in the 1960s, Stamford was placed in South Kesteven, and the new council chose Grantham for its headquarters. Some six or seven hundred years of increasing self-government came to an end. Decisions on all issues relating to Stamford are now taken outside the town, often without any elected representative of the town being present. However sensitively the present council and its officers act (and they *are* aware of Stamford's needs), the 1974 Act represents for Stamford much less self-government, not more.

And the issues are urgent. There is, for instance, the preservation of one of the most valuable of all historic town centres in the country. There are three main threats. First, the main ancient core of the town is largely emptied of residents; the windows of the floors above almost all of the shops stare with vacant eyes on busy streets. Secondly, the traffic problem remains; heavy lorries still tear at the corners, still shake the foundations. And thirdly the modernisation of houses, so much demanded by banks and building societies, is destroying what all the years between have not destroyed, their mediaeval hearts.

Stamford therefore needs loving care and attention. It urgently needs an east-west bypass as much as it needed a north-south one. But if this is seen as a device for Stamford to stay at rest, to avoid change, to preserve fossilised its 'ancient charms', then the future for the town is bleak. For Stamford needs to discover both a role for itself and the means for greater participation in decision-making (perhaps through local community associations and a Development Trust) if it is to recover a sense of self-confidence, a role greater than that of tourist centre or middle class dormitory. And these are problems for Stamfordians to solve, if the politicians and administrators in Grantham and elsewhere will let them. If this book helps them with this process, it will have done much for what is still one of England's most beautiful and alive towns.

Browne's Hospital restored: interior of court.

ABOVE: The almshouses. LEFT: The warden's residence in Broad Street. RIGHT: North Street Baptist Chapel; the 1834 building stands behind this imposing facade of 1900.

View over Stamford to north west, showing open spaces and modern houses
built on land enclosed in the 1870s.

ABOVE: Large houses at west end of Broad Street. BELOW: Girls High
School, High Street, St Martin's.

ABOVE: Rebuilding in Broad Street on a grand scale. LEFT: Mid-Lent fair in Broad Street c1895. RIGHT: Stamford's Power Station on the site of Blashfield's terracotta works on Wharf Road. The terracotta wall can still be seen in the photograph. OPPOSITE: Industry: ABOVE: Blackstone's first building in Broad Street. BELOW: The new industrial works in Broad Street (the site is now the cinema/bingo hall).

LTD. ENGINEERS.
BLACKSTONE & CO.
Messrs BLACKSTONE & Co LTD
NEW SHOWROOMS & WAREHOUSE

ABOVE: Pick delivery van. BELOW: Parade and presentation in Red Lion Square 1895. (SLHS)

ABOVE: Public meeting, Red Lion Square c1900. BELOW: Demolition of the castle to make way for a 'bus station. (MP)

133

Castle demolition. (MP)

The spread of the town after enclosure: ABOVE: the first extension to the town, Tinwell Road; BELOW: large Houses, Tinwell Road 1880s.

135

ABOVE: Smaller houses, Conduit Road. BELOW: Middle class
residences, Casterton Road.

ABOVE: Between-the-wars development, Melbourn Road; BELOW:
one of the new breed of suburban churches, Stamford Free Church.

Sources

As the first chapter shows, Stamford has not lacked its historians. The earliest accounts of the town, are, however, most useful for what they tell us about the period in which they were written rather than in the information they contain concerning the more remote past. Anyone who wishes to delve deeper into the history of this fascinating town should start with the following books:

1. *Early Accounts*
   Richard Butcher, *A Survey and Antiquity of the Town of Stamford* (1646 edition is rare; re-printed in Peck and separately in 1727): useful on the town in the mid-seventeenth century.

   Frances Howgrave, *An Essay on the Ancient and Present State of Stamford* (1726): of limited value; written 'to annoy Peck'.

   Francis Peck, *Antiquarian Annals of Stamford* (1727; reprinted with index and new introduction in 1979): tedious but contains much original material, some of which no longer survives. His other writings, *Desiderata Curiosa* (2 vols., 1732, 1735), include some material as well.

   W. Harrod, *The Antiquities of Stamford and St Martin's* (1785): again useful for the 1780s.

2. *Nineteenth century*
   Thomas Blore's *Account of the Public Schools, Hospitals and other Charitable Foundations of the Borough of Stamford* (1813) set the tone to the century — controversial and polemical but with interesting material.

   The most useful of nineteenth-century writers are John Drakard, *History of Stamford* (1822) and George Burton, *Chronology of Stamford* (1846). Lesser works, such as M. E. C. Walcott, *Memorials of Stamford* (1867) and C. Nevinson *History of Stamford* (1879), are largely derivative.

3. *Modern Accounts*
   The first attempt at a serious history was Alan Rogers (ed.), *The Making of Stamford* (1965), a series of essays.

   B. L. Deed's *History of Stamford School* (1954) has material on a wider range of subjects than its title suggests. *Stamford in 1850,* by E. Hodgkinson and L. Tebbutt (1954) contains some useful items.

   J. W. F. Hill's four volumes on Lincoln, especially the first, *Mediaeval Lincoln* (1948), contains a good deal on Stamford and its Lincolnshire background; so too do *Tudor and Stuart Lincoln* (1956), *Georgian Lincoln* (1966) and *Victorian Lincoln* (1974). The nine volumes so far published in the History of Lincolnshire series are full of material relating to the town and the region in the south of that county.

The Town of Stamford, published by the Royal Commission on Historical Monuments in 1977, has both general essays and a wealth of detailed material.

The publications of the Stamford Archaeological Research Committee and later the South Lincolnshire Archaeological Unit, both their monographs on different aspects of the town and the serial production, *South Lincolnshire Archaeology,* are adding to our knowledge of the town all the time.

From time to time, the Stamford Survey Group has issued reports and papers; more recently, it has begun a journal, *The Stamford Historian,* which contains many articles written by professional and amateur local historians alike. It is the best means of keeping up-to-date as the story of Stamford's past continues to unfold.

4. *Documentary sources*
    Original material lies mostly in the Public Record Office (London) and in the county records offices at Lincoln and Northampton, where the diocesan records also rest. Scattered items relating to Stamford lie elsewhere, from Durham to Kent. The manuscripts in Burghley House are still being listed and are not generally accessible.

In the town, the most useful collections are in the Town Hall, Browne's Hospital and in the various parish chests. The *Stamford Mercury* is a mine of information.

The earliest maps of Stamford (apart from Speed's map of about 1600) are those by Knipe (1833) and Dewhurst and Nicholls (1839).

The Stamford Survey Group has built up an extensive facsimile bank of records relating to Stamford and a large collection of old photographs.

Index

Subscribers
Presentation Copies

1 **Stamford Town Council**

2 **South Kesteven District Council**

3 **Stamford Library**

4 **Lincolnshire Library Service**

5 **Stamford Survey Group**

6 **Lady Victoria Leatham**

7 **Canon J.P. Hoskins**

8 **John Chandler**

9 **Northants Record Office**

10 **Lincolnshire Record Office**

11 Alan Rogers
12 Clive & Carolyn Birch
13 Mrs T.M. Jones
14 Mrs Jill Gibb
15 Mr & Mrs Frank Dyson
16 Rev P.J.M. Bryan
17 S. Gray
18 J.R. Shields
19 B.T.Stephens
20 Lincolnshire Museums
21 P.B. Hemphill
22 G.N. Williamson
23 D.F. Simpson
24 Mr & Mrs J.D. Hill
25 Mr H. Ross
26 M.J.S. Roberts
27 D.J. Codling
28 Ward Hopkin
29 G.M. Flynn
30 C. Forrest
31 J.E.M. Smith
32 C. Davies
33 Mr & Mrs Charles Wide
34 B. Longbottom
35 Mrs B. Wright
36 Peter Chard
37 Mrs E.M. Moment
38 Mr & Mrs D.G. Turner
39 Victoria & Albert Museum
40 David A. Bratton
41 Mr & Mrs T.R. Anderton
42 Miss V.G. Exton
43 Mrs H.M. Tourtel
44 L.H. Millard
45 L.C. Dolby
46 H.M. Rowett
47 Mrs B. Lovelle
48 A.J. Young
49 F.W. Holland
50 M. & C.E. Bell
51 Mrs Joan Innocent
52 Frank E. Curtis

53 Ian J. Curtis
54 Roger A. Curtis
55 Mrs Margery Andrews
56 Miss Catherine Mary Pick
57 G.W. Walker
58 David Newton
59 C.W.H. Aldridge
60 Mrs Jennifer Betts
61 Mrs T.E.R. Branson
62 A.C. Hoyles
63 Ian G. Harris
64 D.J. Barnett
65 / 67 J.H. Chandler
68 P.E. Gosling
69 G.T. Slingsby
70 Mr & Mrs M.R. Atkinson
71 Mr & Mrs S.C. Spencer
72 Colin J. Lawson MSAAT
73 David H. Islip
74 P. Thomas
75 R.A. Wilkins
76 M.J. Hirst
77 Mrs Margaret Kingston
78 Bob Cadman
79 Mrs F.O. Clark
80 E.J.C. Warner
81 Iris Joan White
82 Mrs J.A. Bancroft
83 Mrs J. Rochester
84 Mrs M.E. Howell
85 Gavin Johns
86 E. Woodcock
87 A.L. Lay
88 D.R. Roffe
89 J. Cottingham
90 Mr & Mrs L.J. Facer
91 P. Baxter
92 Mrs M.B. Bridge
93 Mrs S.M. Simpson
94 R.V. Heath

95 A. Fuller
96 Mrs Heydon
97 Mrs Anne Wendy Wheeler
98 J.D. Dolby
99 P.E. Hirst
100 Susan Hirst
101 Andrew Hirst
102 Christopher Hirst
103 J.S. English
104 Sqn Ldr J.W. Davies
105 Miss Alice Essex
106 Lynda & Barry Glover
107 Mrs D.C. Webb
108 T.M. Gale
109 Miss G. Bland
110 Mrs R.F. Earl
111 M.J. Marin
112 Rev M.T. Peach
113 Mrs Audrey M. Green
114 Dr G.A. Beck
115 C.F. Beck
116
117 Mrs B.A. Mutehell
118 Dr L.R. Holt
119 Mrs B. Waterworth
120 R.A. Dodkin
121 Mrs B. Kudlinski
122 J.A. Rowley
123 Mrs G. Riley
124 Miss M. Noble
125 Michael J. Warby
126 Rev Canon E.F. & Mrs Wright
127 Miss Stella G.A. Henriques
128 Mrs E.E. Taylor
129 / 130 W.E. Hayre
131 Mr & Mrs Walker
132 Mrs G.D. Kew
133 Peter Loft
134 R.A. Lilley
135 Brett Culpin

136 Mr & Mrs L.J. Facer
137 Mr & Mrs W. Atherton
138 D. Bond
139 Mrs M.E. Tyler
140 P.J. Baylis
141 Mrs H.M. Stott
142 Mrs H. Eastgate
143 D.A. Smith
144 Mrs E. Heckingbottom
145 Nigel Chubb
146 William Arthur Johnson
147 Paul Ridgway
148 Mrs Jenny Paling
149 Mr & Mrs R.J. Winstanley
150 Roy Grayson
151 Mrs S. Mansbridge
152 Mr & Mrs J.S. Sandercombe
153 Dr D.M. Butler
154 Mrs M. Fairweather
155 Mrs E. Bateson
156 Rev K.P. Lingard
157 G.D. Richardson
158 G.E. Williams
159 Rev & Mrs G.A. Sayers
160 Miss M. Patrick
161 T.W. Fitchett
162 G.W.P. Stretton
163 D. Foreman
164 Mrs J.R. Birkle
165 J.A. Watson
166 Mrs M. Berry
167 Stamford College of Further Education
168 Mrs J. Murray
169 Mrs M. Watts
170 W. Towers
171 Mr & Mrs P.A. Simmons & Zoe
172 Delyth Dronfield
173 Miss E. Hill

174 J.A. Macduff
175 I.N. Sutcliffe
176 J.G. Horn
177 M. Lambkin
178 W.T. Cowan
179 Miss Holly M. Hamill
180 Marigold Lamin
181 Mrs K. Walker
182 G. Hassell
183 A.P. Middleton
184 Mrs L.F. Curtis
185 Mrs Joan Wakefield
186 Mrs Sally Cowley
187 Miss A. Sutherland
188 Mrs Kenneth Grose
189 Stamford High School
191 Owen Franks
192 R.J. Burt
193 B.G. Sells
194 Mrs C. Hewinns-Burdock
195 Mrs Catherine Grose
196 G.M. Acum
197 B. Pollard
198 Miss M. Coles
199 Mr & Mrs M.H. Thomas
200 Stamford Development Committee
201 Sandra D. Smith
202 Leo Kendrick
203 Miss F.J. Hinson
204 Joseph S. Leeton
205 B.B. Kinealy
206 C. Addison
207 Miss B. Murphy
208 Prof J.P. Roberts
209 E.C. Willson
210 J.M. Graham
211 D.K. Brown
212 P.J. Wilmot
213 Elaine Clark
214 M. Bury
215 M.R. Bone
216 R.D. West
217 B.J. Ridley
218 Rev A.J.B. Kettle
219 David Harris
220 T. Debney
221 Mrs C.M. Debney
222 Miss C.M. Hill
223 J.R. & M.M.J. Aylward
224 E. Cooke
225 B. Matthews
226 Miss K. Burton
227 Dr J.A. Derry
228 H.G. Schofield
229 Dr N.R. Seymour

230 Mis J.M. Price
231 Mrs J. Oliver
232 J.L. Barber
233 P.R. Todd
234 Mrs Schofield
235 Mrs Lord
236 M. Hensman
237 Mr Belsham
238 Mr Leveritt
239 A.G. Severn
240 D.K. Allen
241 M.G. Kitchen
242 R. Drewery
243 R.B. Holland
244 David S. Jones
245 Mrs J.P. Foster
246 F. Felstead
247 G.E. Sendall
248 Harry Warby
249 Mr & Mrs K.A. Schmidt
250 Mrs W. Last
251
252 Miss E.K. Stokes
253 James Cliff
254 Miss S. English
255 Mr & Mrs S.P. Johnson
256 E.H. Berry
257
258 A.W. Ingram
259 K.P. Ford
260 C.A. Harwood
261 Charles Wright
262 P.G. Dowdall MBE
263 Mrs K.A. Lord
264 The Library, The University of Leicester
265 Mrs D.L. Phipps
266 Eric C.W. Trunill
267 Museum of Lincolnshire Life
268 Mrs C.M. Wilson
269 P.J.K. Stonehouse
270 C.J. & B.M. Pearson
271 Rev A.J.C. Kettle
272 J. Wallack
273 L.G. Moden
274 Jane Clarke
275 Mrs J. Crawford
276
277 D. Winter
278 Mrs D. Brown
279 D.M. Brereton
280 Michael & Diana Honeybone
281 Mrs B. Lytwynchuk
282 Noel Jones

283 Mrs M.E. Bartle
284 Lincolnshire Library
348 Service
349 Peter Hargreaves
350 Christine & Tony Powell
351 Mrs Alice Joyner
352 Mrs A.J. Bawden
353 Mrs Thelma Bell
354 Mrs G.G.M. Bradley
355 Bluecoat CP School, Stamford
356 Mrs M.L. Cane
357 Mrs Pat Barlow
358 Alec Ronald Burt
359 Paul White
360 John Culshaw
361 St Augustine's RC Primary School
362 Mr & Mrs T. Crowden
363 Mr & Mrs D.G. Pillar
364 Stamford Education & Training Officer RAF Oakham
365 Mrs M.J. Graham
366 C.P. Wright
367 G.H. Boyle
368 Garry M. Till
369 Derick H. Fox
370 Ms F.M. Gillespie
371 G.E. Griffin
372 David Newton
373 J. Wallace
374 Miss J.M. Taylor
375 Miss J.O. Farndell
376 Mrs N. Edmonds
377 Mr & Mrs I.R. Walters
378 G.C. Johns
379 David Kaye
380 Joyce E. Ekins
381 Kenneth Lewis
382
385 Leicestershire Libraries & Information Service
386 N.I. Browning
387 Mrs Isabella Burbeck
388 M.D. Grimes
389 K.A. Cole
390 F.H. Riley
391 The Librarian, Stamford School
392 B.L. Leete
393 Eric Ladbrook
394
395 J.A. McNab
396 T.E. Merriman
397 T.A. Burrows
398 T.E. Tyers
399 Stamford Development Committee

400 P.J. Watts
401 S. Gray
402 M.F. English
403 Miss Kathleen Burton
404 Dr J.A. Derry
405 Mrs G.E. Hill
406 J.S. Thurlby
407 Mrs E.S. Dean
408 John Tetlow
409 Mrs G. Lemon
410 Ian R. Broughton
411 Mrs Margaret Sims
412 C. Taylor
413 John Currall
414 Robert Andrew Paterson
415 P.L. Brunnen
416 Mrs M.I. Beasley
417 Mrs E.M. Serjeant
418 J.R. Shelford
419 H.C. Clarke
420 B. Brown
421 Miss P. Meredith
422 N.I. Browning
423 R. Freear
424 Mrs G. Flanagan
425 Dr A.F.M. Little
426 T.W. Fenton
427
428 John Atkins
429 Prudence Levitt
430 J.S. Thurby
431 W.I. Graham
432 J.H. Woodman
433 E.C. Stanley
434 Mrs B. Flint
435 J.P. Dorrington
436 F.N. Flanders
437 P.W. Bearne
438 L.A. Knapp
439 K.R. Jones
440
443 John Colley Carter
444 Mrs M.M. Goodwin
445 P.S.Y. Jessop
446 E.L. Thornley
447 Mrs B. Rose
448 M.J. Hinson
449 Judith Spelman
450 M.J. & E.I. Tubb
451 Mrs F.L. Fryer
452 Christopher C. Hunt, BA
453 J.F. Smith
454 S. Smith
455 David Billings
456 Charles E. Bray

Remaining names unlisted.

Peace and tranquility in Barn Hill: for how long?

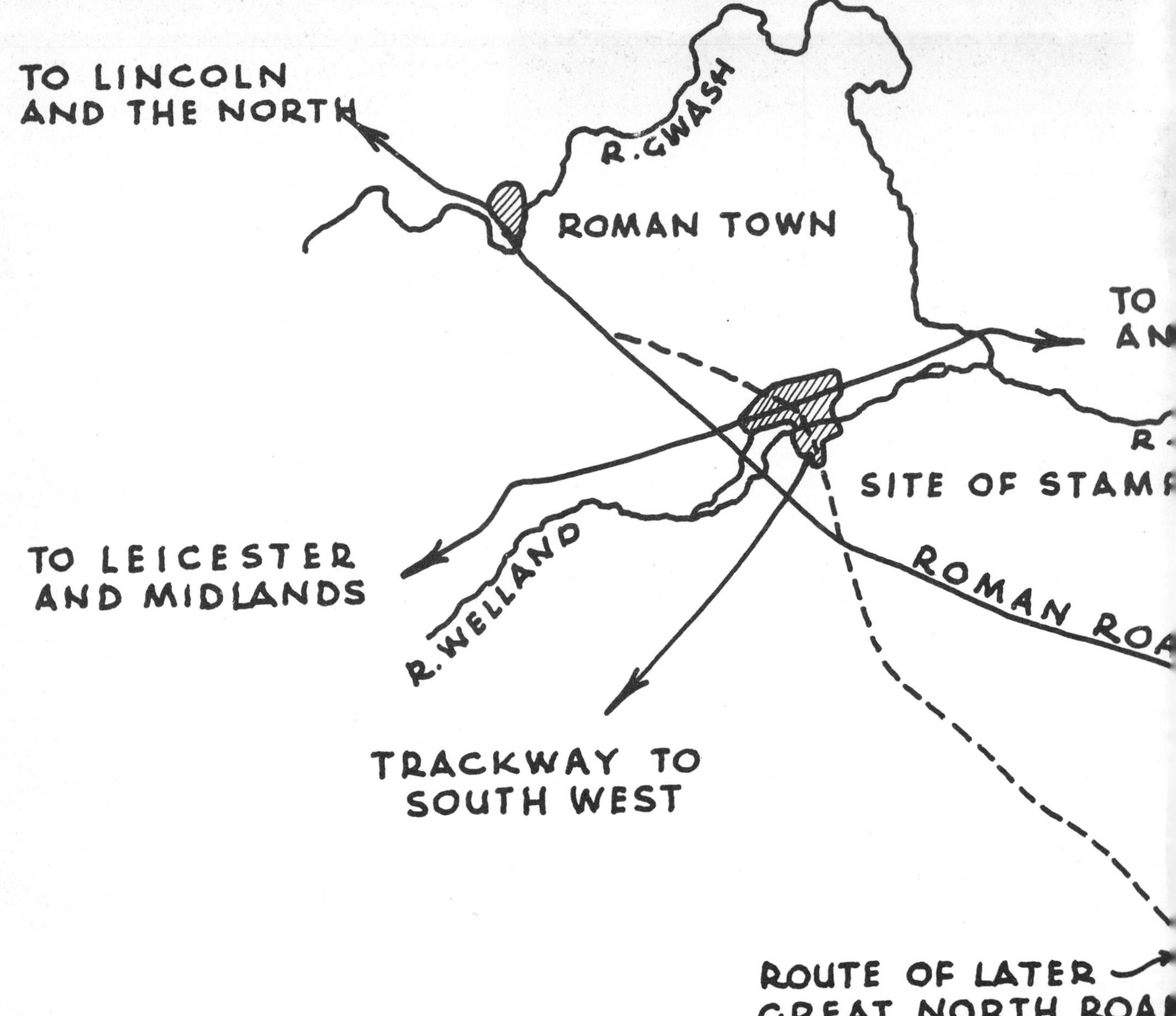

TO LINCOLN
AND THE NORTH
R. GWASH
ROMAN TOWN
TO
AN
R.
SITE OF STAMF
TO LEICESTER
AND MIDLANDS
R. WELLAND
ROMAN ROA
TRACKWAY TO
SOUTH WEST
ROUTE OF LATER
GREAT NORTH ROAD